Like a Knife

Like a Knife
Ideology and Genre in Contemporary Chinese Popular Music

Andrew F. Jones

East Asia Program
Cornell University
Ithaca, NY 14853-7601

The *Cornell East Asia Series* publishes manuscripts on a wide variety of scholarly topics pertaining to East Asia. Manuscripts are published on the basis of camera-ready copy provided by the volume author or editor.

Inquiries should be addressed to Editorial Board, Cornell East Asia Series, East Asia Program, Cornell University, 140 Uris Hall, Ithaca, New York 14853.

©1992 Andrew F. Jones
ISSN 8756-5293
ISBN 0-939657-57-0

CONTENTS

Acknowledgements   vii

Introduction: "Like a Knife"   1

1. Ideology and Genre in Chinese Popular Music   7

2. Ideological Struggle in *Tongsu* Music   35

3. *Tongsu* Music as a Genre   65

4. Rock Music as a Genre   91

5. Cui Jian and the Ideology of Chinese Rock Music   115

Conclusion: "We Dedicate this Knife to You"   145

Appendix: Selected *Tongsu* and Rock Song Lyrics   151

Bibliography   165

Discography   177

ACKNOWLEDGEMENTS

This study originates from an undergraduate thesis presented to the Department of East Asian Languages and Civilizations at Harvard University in 1991. Without the generous financial support of Harvard's Center for International Affairs, the research I conducted for this study in Beijing during the Summer of 1990 would not have been possible. I am especially grateful for the support of the Center for the Study of Non-Violent Sanctions.

Many scholars and friends at Harvard provided invaluable help and guidance. Catherine Yeh was an able, enthusiastic, and supportive adviser, whose sense of intellectual adventure kept me both inspired and on my toes throughout the writing process. For over a year, Kathryn Lowry reviewed my drafts, urged me to define my terms, handed down directives, and pointed the way towards new and productive avenues of thought and analysis. Stephen Owen's insights on song lyrics and performance were consistently stimulating. Graeme Boone gave me invaluable lessons on how the music works as *music*. Throughout the writing process, Cherry Chan helped clear up difficult points in translation, and arranged for the latest CD's from Hong Kong to be delivered to my doorstep.

For making my stay in Beijing in 1990 a happy and productive one, I am indebted to the efforts of Han Xin'an. Without his collaboration, much of the research presented here would not have been accomplished. Professor Zhong Zilin of the Central Conservatory of Music was unstintingly generous with his time and energy. Finally, I would like to acknowledge the efforts of An Dong, Cui Jian, Dong Dong, Liu Xiaosong, Wang Qun, and Zhu Xiaomin.

My deepest gratitude goes to my mother, Franka Jones, for her love, support, and newspaper clippings.

Finally, this book is dedicated to all the musicians in Beijing who both inspired and actively collaborated with me to make this project a reality.

INTRODUCTION

"LIKE A KNIFE"

If Western rock is like a flood, then Chinese rock is
like a knife. We dedicate this knife to you.

—Cui Jian, prefacing a
performance of his song "Like
a Knife" at Beijing Exhibition
Hall, March 12, 1989.

On June 4, 1989, the People's Republic of China's 'new era' (*xin
shiqi*) of economic reform and modernization temporarily fell to pieces over
the issue of just what kind of modernity China was advancing towards. In
the streets and squares of Beijing, students and workers had demonstrated for
six weeks for a modern China that would allow for a greater degree of
political liberty and personal freedom. Their movement was suppressed by
the People's Liberation Army; the principles of the Chinese Communist
Party (CCP) held sway for the moment.

In the months that followed the crackdown, the CCP embarked on
the task of 'raising morale,' of winning back the hearts and minds of the
Chinese people through ideological persuasion. Tight restrictions were
imposed on cinematic and literary production. A campaign against
pornography was set into motion. Popular songs about romantic love or
personal emotions were banned from the nation's television screens. In the
spring of 1990, a massive propaganda campaign to promote the upcoming
11th Asian Games (a regional sports competition modelled on the Olympic
games) in Beijing inundated every medium of mass communication with
nationalist and socialist sentiment.

Popular music played an integral role in this effort to raise public
morale. Songs in praise of the Asian Games, produced and promoted by the
state-run popular music industry, flooded the popular music market and the

1

mass media. "The Valiant Spirit of Asia," a song produced by some of China's most famous songwriters and singers, was sold in every record store, featured on every televised pop music show, sung at every concert, and poured out of every train and subway public address system. Even if you did not like its evocation of a world in which the people of every nation unhesitatingly contended to embrace a wealthy, modern, socialist China where the Tiananmen massacre had never happened, its melody was catchy. And unless you stayed inside with the television and the radio unplugged for four months in a row, you were bound to get hooked.

Hosting the Asian Games, of course, was an enormously expensive affair, and the CCP was hard-pressed to make ends meet. Cui Jian, China's foremost rock singer, was enlisted to undertake a concert tour of eight major Chinese cities in an effort to raise one million *yuan* (about $400,000 U.S.) for the sporting events in Beijing. He was, in many ways, an unlikely choice. Cui Jian was affiliated not with the state-run popular music industry, but with an underground rock subculture centered in Beijing. At the height of the 1987 campaign against "bourgeois liberalization," he had been denounced as subversive, and banned from giving large-scale concerts. He was a favorite among Chinese college students, as well as among disenfranchised unemployed and self-employed youth. His song "I Have Nothing" (*Yiwu suoyou*, 1986), had become an anthem of the democracy movement, during which he had performed live at Tiananmen Square for more than a thousand students staging a hunger strike.

All of this, of course, ensured that the tour would be an enormous success. As the tour progressed, Cui's performances became increasingly incendiary. As Cui blindfolded himself with a red cloth—unmistakably symbolic of the CCP—his adoring fans (many of whom had paid the equivalent of several month's salary for tickets on the black market) broke into rebellious shouts, cheers, and frenzied dances. Such demonstrations of discontent quickly led CCP officials to cut the tour short. Once again, Cui Jian was prohibited from giving large-scale concerts.

In likening Chinese rock music to a knife, Cui Jian suggests that his music—in contrast to the blunt ubiquity of its Western counterpart—remains pointed enough to "cut away at social and political problems."[1] In this study I propose that not only Cui Jian's brand of underground rock music, but also the popular music industry that produced "The Valiant

---

[1] Interview with Cui Jian, Beijing, July 31, 1990.

Spirit of Asia," are deeply engaged in the larger struggles over cultural and political meaning that came to a head with the Tiananmen movement of 1989. As the narrative of the role of popular music in promoting the Asian Games attests, the popular music of China's 'new era' has been, and continues to be, wielded by musicians, audiences, critics, and CCP officials alike as a means of furthering their own ideological ends.

Chinese popular music is less a mere adjunct to leisure than a battlefield on which ideological struggle is waged. The CCP has consistently endeavored to engineer the pleasures of popular music to the end of retaining power, bolstering their own ideological legitimacy, and making money. Popular songwriters, working within the state-run popular music industry, have attempted to use popular songs as forums for controversial reflections on the nature of Chinese culture and Chinese modernity. Rock musicians, operating outside the strictures of 'mainstream' popular music, have yoked their music to the service of an oppositional ideology of individualism, and anti-feudalism.

Clearly, the knife cuts in many ways. Popular music has functioned as an arena in which many different voices have attempted to speak for 'the people,' to gain the "power to construct authoritative definitions of social situations and legitimate interpretations of social needs."[2] In this book, I contend that these constructions of *meaning* in Chinese popular music—whether on the part of musicians, fans, or critics— are intimately related to constructions of *genre*. By genre, I do not mean categorizations based primarily on musical style or lyrical content. Instead, I use the term to indicate the whole constellation of institutional structures, activities, individual sensibilities, discursive practices and ideological aims by which any given type of popular music is produced, performed, disseminated, discussed, and used by its audiences.

In this sense, Chinese popular music is not so much a knife, but a double-edged sword. Popular music is divided into two broadly-defined genres: officially-sanctioned popular music (*tongsu yinyue*), and underground rock music (*yaogun yinyue*). These two genres are produced, distributed, and performed in fundamentally divergent ways, and discussed by musicians, fans, and critics in altogether different terms. *Tongsu* music and rock music are further differentiated by distinctive patterns of musical style and lyrical content. Finally, the sensibilities and ideological aims of

---

[2] Nancy Fraser, *Unruly Practices: Power, Discourse, and Gender in Contemporary Social Theory,* (Minneapolis: University of Minnesota Press, 1989), 6.

musicians working within each genre are profoundly different and often mutually contentious.

More important, these genres have acted as vehicles for the articulation of ideology in disparate ways. *Tongsu* music in the 'new era' has served two different functions. First, the majority of *tongsu* music is propaganda; its production, distribution, performance, and content is circumscribed by the ideological imperatives of the CCP. Even so, as the very fact that a musician like Cui Jian was recruited to redress the CCP's financial woes indicates, ideological orthodoxy in the 'new era' has often fallen prey to the demands placed on the state by economic reform. I argue that economic reform and liberalization have cleared new, and hotly contested, discursive spaces for popular songwriters and critics. In a literal sense, this discursive space is the nationalized mass media through which *tongsu* music reaches its audiences. In recent years, the mass media have served as a forum for a larger movement of "cultural self-reflection" (*wenhua fansi*) and "roots-seeking" (*xungen yishi*). *Tongsu* music has played a complex and integral role in these debates by figuring contending visions of Chinese culture and its modernization in terms of individual desires and private life.

While *tongsu* music is characterized by its engagement with the mass culture of the 'new era,' rock music has largely been relegated to its subcultural margins. Participants in this rock subculture share a coherent ideology of cultural opposition. Rock musicians and fans strive to release themselves from the oppression and hypocrisy that they believe is endemic to China's 'feudal culture' by means of a faith in individualism and authenticity. This subcultural ideology has both been influenced by and exercised a profound influence upon mass culture and the public sphere which it circumscribes. The sensibilities of rock musicians represent a radicalization of many of the notions championed by "roots-seekers." The oppositional energies of rock music, in turn, have been appropriated by a burgeoning youth culture—composed of college students and private entrepreneurs—as a means for the articulation of political dissent.

Methodology and Structure

I first became interested in Chinese popular music as a visiting student at Beijing University in 1988-89. Popular music seemed to be speaking to its audiences in many contradictory tongues, and audiences seemed to be using the music as a way to reflect on their own lives, to understand the cultural dilemmas faced by a rapidly modernizing nation, and sometimes, to talk back to the authorities. I was intrigued by the emergence of "cultural self-reflection" in the "Northwest Wind" (a *tongsu* style that fuses Chinese folk music with disco), puzzled by the seemingly inexplicable craze among Beijing's youth for "jail songs" that related the woes of convicts and rusticated youth, and inspired by the adoption of Cui Jian's "I Have Nothing" as a kind of unofficial anthem for the democracy movement. With the aid of a grant from Harvard's Center for International Affairs, I returned to China in the summer of 1990 in hopes of discovering a pattern that could link all these phenomena into a coherent intellectual whole.

This book is the product of that effort. In June and July of 1990, I conducted interviews in Beijing with approximately twenty rock musicians, *tongsu* singers, *tongsu* songwriters, and music critics. All interviews were conducted in Chinese; eight of the interviews were accomplished in collaboration with a Chinese scholar affiliated with the Central Conservatory of Music and the journal *People's Music* (*Renmin yinyue*), Han Xin'an. The perceptions, experiences, and insights related to me by these interviewees form of the backbone of my argument about ideology and genre in Chinese popular music. In addition, I refer throughout the study to Chinese critical writings on popular music, *tongsu* and rock song lyrics, recordings, and rock and *tongsu* performances I witnessed both in 1988-89, and during the summer of 1990.

Because of the complexity of the topic, and the paucity of English language scholarship in the field, I have endeavored to present a multi-faceted portrait of the dynamics of genre and ideology in Chinese popular music. My approach is multi-disciplinary, incorporating sociological, musicological, and textual criticism. Throughout the work, I engage in dialogue with many of the ideas of Western scholars of mass culture, social theory, and cultural studies in an effort to place the realities of the Chinese music scene in a larger theoretical framework.

The book is divided into five chapters. In chapter one, I define terms such as "popular music," "genre," and "ideology," and go on to situate the popular music of the 'new era' within the context of the seventy-year history of Chinese popular music. Finally, I detail the divisions between *tongsu* music and rock music and present Liu Suola's "A Superfluous Story" as a powerful model for the interpretation of generic differences in Chinese popular music, and the struggles that underlie them. Chapters two and three portray the way in which *tongsu* music is produced, performed, and discussed by its singers and songwriters, and analyze the genre's role in the articulation of ideology. Chapters four and five are devoted to a parallel discussion of rock music.

Note on Romanization, and a Disclaimer

All Chinese words are romanized according to the official *pinyin* system. All translations from the Chinese are my own, unless otherwise noted.

Finally, I would like to add a short disclaimer. Although imported popular music (particularly that of Hong Kong and Taiwan) has played a seminal role in the development of Chinese popular music since 1978, and continues to command a substantial share of the Chinese popular music market, I have chosen to restrict my discussion to popular music produced within the borders of the People's Republic of China.

IDEOLOGY AND GENRE IN CHINESE POPULAR MUSIC

Foundations: What is Popular Music?

What is popular music? What form does it take in contemporary China? In the face of a bewildering array of possible approaches to these problems, it is important to carve out a working definition of exactly what is denoted by the term itself. In Western and non-Western nations alike, the development of popular music, in marked contrast to classical and regional folk musics, has come hand in hand with the commodification of economies, the development of technology and the mass media, and urbanization. In non-Western contexts, popular music has grown out of the acculturation and synthesis of Western musical culture with indigenous forms.

The editors of *Popular Music* have noted that:

> ...popular music is typical of societies with a relatively highly developed division of labor and a clear distinction between producers and consumers, in which cultural products are created largely by professionals, sold in a mass market and reproduced through mass media.[1]

The use of the term "cultural product" is telling, for popular music exists simultaneously as a market commodity, a form of secular entertainment, and an element of a larger socio-political and cultural system. In socialist as well as capitalist nations, popular music "ultimately entails commodification."[2] The production and distribution of popular music requires capital investment for instruments, recording equipment, manufacturing facilities, and skilled workers. In order to recoup the

---

[1] Editors of Popular Music, *Popular Music* 1. As cited in Peter Manuel, *Popular Musics of the Non-Western World*, (New York: Oxford University Press, 1989), 2.
[2] Manuel, 15.

necessary capital outlay, record companies (be they the media conglomerates of capitalist nations or the nationalized production units of socialist countries) must direct their products towards the mass market.

The entrance of popular music into the mass market is achieved primarily through the mass media. Indeed, dissemination through radio, television, film, and recordings is often cited as popular music's most distinctive feature. Thus, in contrast to both classical and folk musics, the production, performance, and dissemination of popular music are all inseparable from the use of modern Western technologies. In China, for instance, cinema has served as the principal medium for the dissemination of popular music since the 1920's; only in the past ten years has this role been partially supplanted by other imported technologies, the television and the audio-cassette player.

Popular music's close links with the mass market and the technology of the mass media create two important corollaries. First, popular music is urban music; it usually flourishes in the populous, industrialized areas that are able to provide the economic resources and technological expertise essential to its continued existence. Its performers and audiences are predominantly urban in origin (although with the spread of television and audio-cassette player ownership, its influence has begun to extend to China's rural audiences). Second, popular music, as opposed to various regional folk musics, is usually national in character. In contemporary China, the vast majority of popular music is produced in a few major urban centers (Beijing, Tianjin, Shanghai, Guangzhou). This music is, in turn, broadcast nationwide by state-owned radio and television stations, featured in nationally distributed films, and sold throughout the country on audio-cassette by a network of national and provincial audio-visual publishers. The popular music industry thus participates in a larger system of national mass culture that is comprised of the television, film, radio, and print industries, and linked by common state ownership and the use of a standardized national language (*putonghua*).[3] The 'underground' rock music that is an important focus of this study is a notable exception, for it is routinely denied access to the most important of these nationalized mass media, television.[4]

---

[3] For a study of China's television, broadcasting and print media, see Won Ho Chang, *Mass Media in China: The History and the Future*, (Ames: Iowa State University Press, 1989), 151-229.

[4] Another partial exception to this rule is popular music performed in Cantonese. The market for Cantonese pop is obviously concentrated on (but not entirely restricted to) the Cantonese-speaking areas of Guangdong province and its environs. Chinese mass culture since 1956

9

There is an important sense in which popular music is also necessarily an international phenomena, for its development in non-Western societies has been bound up with musical syncretism and the acculturation of Western musical forms.[5] In China, Western harmonies, American popular song form, and Western instrumentation (including the use of pianos, electric guitars, violins, drums and synthesizers) have been acculturated to such an extent that "national elements may consist only of language and such features as a preference for pentatonic melodies."[6] From its beginnings in the late 1920's to the present day, Chinese popular music has incorporated indigenous folk melodies and instruments (including the *dizi*, a transverse bamboo flute, *zheng*, a zither,and the *suona,* a single reed trumpet) into syncretic popular styles largely predicated on borrowings from the West (jazz, classical, disco, and rock). As Peter Manuel reminds us in his survey of non-Western popular musics, musical syncretism and acculturation "cannot be fully understood independently of the legacy of of the colonial past and the imperialist present."[7] This fact, in turn, is central to understanding the ways in which the development of Chinese popular music has consistently been situated at the highly politicized cusp between the importation of Western technology and Western cultural imperialism, and the complex set of Chinese responses to this encroachment.

The Development of Popular Music in China

The 30's was a laid-back melody
The 40's a tender threnody
The 50's had that vigorous feel
As all the nation smelted steel
The 60's sang "going down to the country"
The 70's model operas were revolutionary
The 80's was breakdance but that's not all
There was a fever for rock and roll
Still there's many songs to sing
What's the 90's gonna bring?[8]

---

has made "rare concessions" to speakers of dialects like Cantonese; and the use of *putonghua* has been enforced expressly as a means of linguistic and cultural standardization. See Paul Clark, *Chinese Cinema: Culture and Politics Since 1949,* (Cambridge: Cambridge University Press, 1987), 56-62.
[5] Manuel, 19-23. For an exhaustive discussion of this issue, see Bruno Nettl, *The Western Impact on World Music,* (New York: Schirmer Books, 1985).
[6] Manuel, 221.
[7] Manuel, 22.
[8] Xie Chengqiang, music and lyrics, "Jiushi niandai zenmeyang" [What's the nineties gonna bring?], Linda Jaivin, trans., "It's Only Rock 'n Roll but China Likes It", *Asian Wall Street*

Chinese popular music has been pressed to the service of various (and often contending) political ideologies and social movements throughout the course of its seventy-year history. Indeed, the development of popular music itself can be read as a kind of shadow history of the complex political struggles of twentieth-century China. Each successive popular music genre in China has been linked, either by its creators or by later commentators, with one of the many combatting ideological positions underlying those struggles. The earliest form of popular music in China, 'yellow music,' is indelibly associated with Western imperialism and bourgeois ideology. The leftist mass music (*qunzhong yinyue*) of the 1930's and 1940's drew its inspiration from a range of nationalist, anti-imperialist and socialist ideologies. The revolutionary song (*geming gequ*) of the 1950's sprang directly from the ideological imperatives of China's communist revolution, while the revolutionary operas (*geming geju*) of the 1960's and 70's were the result of the efforts of the Gang of Four to school the Chinese people in Maoist ideologies of class struggle and 'cultural revolution.' In this sense, the pervasive use of popular music as an instrument of ideological struggle in the 'new era,' and the central role played by genre in shaping the nature of those struggles, is less a novelty than a testament to historical continuity.

Shanghai in the late 1920's was fertile ground for the development of a commodified, syncretic popular music disseminated through the mass media. The city was the bulwark of imperialist encroachment into China, and consequently the most cosmopolitan and heavily industrialized Chinese metropolis of the time. In addition, Shanghai was the center of China's mass media and entertainment industries. By the mid-twenties, Shanghai was home to over one hundred film production companies, several record companies, and innumerable nightclubs and brothels. At the same time, Shanghai was a center of nationalist, anti-imperialist, and communist political thought and activity, particularly in the wake of the Japanese occupation of Manchuria in 1932. All of these factors played a part in shaping the high degree of politicization that became (and remains) a basic dynamic in the production, consumption, and criticism of Chinese popular music.

Since the ascendence to power of the Chinese Communist Party in 1949, the popular music that arose out of Shanghai in the late 1920's and

Journal, October 12, 1990. The translated lyrics derive from a recent compilation of Chinese popular music, *Fantian fudi : Zhongguo xin yinyue xilie zhi er* [The world is overthrown: Chinese new waves volume two], Yongsheng yinyue chuban youxian gongsi SMC 90002, 1990. Xie, a native of Guangzhou, is one of the few Chinese rock singers based outside of Beijing.

early 1930's has been almost universally denigrated as "yellow" or "pornographic" music (*huangse yinyue*), both for its association with the heterodox sexual pleasures of city's thriving underworld of brothels and nightclubs, and with the "financial and literal prostitution [of China] at the hands of the imperialist powers and the native elites."[9] "Yellow music" is principally linked to the work of a Shanghai composer named Li Jinhui who in 1927 turned from the composition of "children's music" (*ertong yinyue*) to popular songs (*liuxing gequ*) like "Sister, I Love You" (*Meimei wo ai ni*), "Peach Blossom River" (*Taohua jiang*), and "Express Train" (*Tebie kuaiche*).[10] From 1927 to 1936, Li's activities included writing film scores (from which many popular tunes were extracted), recording hundreds of records for foreign corporations like RCA/Victor (*Shengli Changpian Gongsi*) and EMI (*Baidai Changpian Gongsi*), and organizing his own "Bright Moon Song and Dance Troupe" (*Mingyue Gewutuan*).[11] This music was disseminated throughout China (and Southeast Asia) by means of film, radio, and records, and gained a particularly large following among Shanghai's burgeoning middle classes. Li's music was essentially a kind of sinified jazz which fused Western instrumentation and harmony with largely pentatonic Chinese folk melodies. Its lyrical content was restricted to romantic themes in keeping with the tastes of the city's urbanized petit-bourgeoisie, and vocal styles tended to reflect this lyrical, 'effeminate' quality.[12]

The second wave of Chinese popular music developed in close conjunction with the work of Shanghai's leftist film-makers, and signalled the explicit politicization of Chinese popular music in opposition to Li's brand of 'yellow music.' Between 1933 and 1937, progressive film companies like Mingxing, Lianhua, and Yihua produced a series of films that realistically treated such issues as the threat of imperialist domination, the War of Resistance to Japan, and the difficulties of the urban proletariat.[13] The title songs of films portraying the vicissitudes of Shanghai working-class life under foreign domination like *Street Angel*

---

[9] Manuel, 223.

[10] Liang Maochun, "Dui woguo liuxing yinyue lishi de sikao"[Thoughts on the history of Chinese popular music], *Renmin yinyue*, 1988/7, 32-4.

[11] In 1935 alone, Li recorded forty records on the American RCA/Victor label. His song and dance troupe toured as far afield as Singapore, and featured many of the leading popular singers of the day including Zhou Xuan, Yan Hua, and others. Liang, 32.

[12] Liang, 33.

[13] Clark, 9-15.

(*Malu tianshi*) and *Fifth Brother Wang* (*Wang Laowu*) gained wide distribution and popularity.[14]

In terms of musical style, personnel, and means of distribution, this new genre of socially-conscious popular music overlapped considerably with its "yellow music" precursors; many of the most prominent leftist songwriters and singers had gotten their start in Li Jinhui's Bright Moon Song and Dance Troupe, and the records were still being produced by companies like EMI and RCA/Victor. In short, these film songs were distinguished not by their musical style—which adopted Li's fusion of Western harmony and instrumentation with pentatonic melodies without significant alteration—but by ideology. The work of progressive filmmakers and composers like Xia Yan, Tian Han, and Nie Er reflected the realization that the enormous power of the mass media could be harnessed in the effective use of popular music as a instrument for the propagation of anti-imperialist, anti-Japanese sentiment.

This effort, however, was by no means unambiguous or univocal. Instead, and this theme will become increasingly important in examining the popular music of the 1980's, popular music was rapidly becoming a discursive space in which various ideologies contended for a measure of dominance. This phenomena is embodied in the figure of the professional songwriter, Liu Lei'an. Liu was the author of both the progressive, anti-imperialist anthem "The Ballad of the Great Wall" (*Changcheng yao*), and a song that, while still enjoying considerable popularity, is often attacked as the epitome of the depravity and decadence of "yellow music" by post-1949 critics: "When Is He Coming Back Again?" (*Heri jun zailai*).[15]

The period of the War of Resistance against Japan and the ensuing civil war between the Nationalist (KMT) and Communist (CCP) parties (1937-49) witnessed the heightened politicization and fragmentation of Chinese popular music. In Japanese-occupied areas (including Manchuria and Shanghai), popular music was often produced by the invading army expressly as a tool of ideological persuasion. Liang Maochun, in a recent essay on popular music history, cites a spate of popular songs lauding the

---

[14] Both films were produced in 1937. *Street Angel* featured the songs "Tianya genü" [The singing girl at the end of the earth] and "Ji siji ge" [Song of the four seasons], performed by the most popular female singer of the era, Zhou Xuan, and composed by Jia Luting in collaboration with the noted leftist writer and filmmaker Tian Han. The songs were based on southern Chinese folk material. "Fifth Brother Wang" was composed by Ren Guang, and is notable for the colloquialism of its lyrical content. Liang praises these songs for their "clear national style and progressive ideological thought." Liang, 33.

[15] As of August 1990, this song (as interpreted by the Taiwanese singer Deng Lijun) was still officially banned in the P.R.C. Deng Lijun, *Greatest Hits, Vol. 3*, Polydor Records 3199-321.

13

"New Manchuria" (*Xin Manzhouguo*) and the "Greater East Asian Co-Prosperity Sphere" (*Dongya gongcun*) that were popularized by the Chinese-born Japanese singer Li Xianglan.[16] Following the defeat of Japan in 1945, Shanghai once again began producing "yellow music" tunes like "Song of Tonight" (*Jinye qu*), "Enchanting Lipstick" (*Zuiren de kouhong*), and "Kiss Me All Over" (*Chuchu wen*). These kinds of songs contended for popularity with the subtle social satire of leftist songwriters like Chen Gexin. In songs like "The Lady in the Pedicab" (*Sanlunche shang de xiaojie*), Chen and a group of four other songwriters sought to revive the themes of social injustice prevalent in the songs of the early 1930's in reaction to what they perceived as the decadence and irrelevance of the majority of popular music content.[17]

At the same time, a very different musical tradition was arising in the inland areas already under Communist Party (CCP) control. Here, musicians who had been active in the progressive film industry of the late 1920's and early 1930's were forging a new, explicitly socialist genre of music commonly referred to as "revolutionary song" (*geming gequ*) or "mass music" (*qunzhong yinyue*). This music owed less to jazz and Chinese folk melodies than to European martial music and romanticism. The work of the two major composers in this genre, Nie Er and Xian Xinghai, continue to exert profound influence on the popular music of post-1949 China.[18]

With the victory of the CCP over the Nationalists in 1949, the musical life of the Chinese mainland was radically reorganized.[19] The production, performance, and distribution of all forms of music were nationalized. In accordance with the widely influential cultural policies first articulated by Mao Zedong at the Yan'an Conference on Art and Literature, post-1949 Chinese music was unabashedly charged with the task of propagating Maoist ideals of class struggle, revolutionary fervor, and self-abnegation in the face of the demands, ideals, and authority of the CCP.[20]

[16] Liang, 33.

[17] Liang, 34. The other four songwriters were Li Jinguang, Tiao Mei, Liang Leyin, and Yan Gongshang.

[18] Nie Er, the composer of China's national anthem, "The March of the Volunteers," actually began his career as a member of Li Jinhui's Bright Moon Song and Dance Troupe. Liang, 32. For a discussion of revolutionary songs (*geming gequ*), see Isabel Wong, "*Geming Gequ*: Songs for the Education of the Masses." In Bonnie MacDougall, ed., *Popular Chinese Literature and Performing Arts in the People's Republic of China 1949-1979*, (Berkeley: University of California Press, 1982), 112-16.

[19] Manuel, 229.

[20] McDougall, Bonnie, *Mao Zedong's Talks at the Yan'an Conference on Literature and Art*, (Ann Arbor: University of Michigan Press, 1980).

Musical production was (and at least nominally remains) restricted to the task of propagating ideology, of serving the needs of the workers, peasants, and soldiers, insofar as those needs were perceived and mandated by the CCP itself.

"Yellow music" was an early casualty of this kind of cultural policy; by the time of the Anti-Rightist Movement of 1957, the prewar tradition of romantic popular song (*shuqing gequ*) that it represented had been effectively eliminated.[21] In its stead, the kind of revolutionary songs and mass music that had been pioneered by figures like Nie Er and Xian Xinghai in the 1940's were enshrined by the CCP as the sole legitimate form of popular musical expression.[22] This institutionalization of mass music represented, in one sense, the culmination of the kind of ideological struggles exemplified by the work of Liu Lei'an. The CCP's imposition of tight control over every aspect of musical production in China effectively left no room for argument, for the ideological contention that had characterized the popular music of the 1930's and 1940's.

Arguably, popular music as such ceased to exist by the late 1950's. Mass music exhibited many of the characteristics of popular music: dissemination through the mass media (particularly film and radio), syncretism in musical style (often featuring folk and traditional operatic melodies revamped for western symphonic orchestration reminiscent of both martial music and composers like Rimsky-Korsakov).[23] Significantly, however, it was neither aimed primarily at urban audiences nor was it strictly speaking a participant in a commodity economy. Its popularity was less a product of market demands than of the marriage of ideological concerns and bureaucratic control of the mass media.[24]

---

[21] Cheng Yun, "Zhongguo dangdai tongsu yinyue huanshi lu" [An overview of contemporary Chinese popular music], *Renmin yinyue*, 1988/2, 3. Liang argues that "yellow music" continued to develop in exile in Hong Kong and Taiwan. In his view, Hong Kong and Taiwanese popular music represents a clear continuation of the tradition established between 1927 and 1949, which "broke back into the mainland" following the relaxation of cultural policy of the late 1970's and early 1980's. While the popular music of these two areas did exert great influence on the resurgence of popular music in the mainland, it remains unclear to what extent later Hong Kong and Taiwanese popular music can be seen as a direct descendent of "yellow music." Liang, 32.

[22] Regional folk music and opera continued to be performed by state-run song and dance troupes throughout the nation, but its lyrical content was usually altered to accommodate the CCP's ideological agenda.

[23] Manuel, 230.

[24] This is not to suggest that mass music did not possess genuine popularity in the sense of being enjoyed by the people. I am simply stressing that the enormity of the structural (in terms of means of production) and ideological differences between mass music and its popular pre-war precedents renders the term "popular music" problematic.

The subordination of mass music to the demands of ideology reached its height during the tumultuous decade of the Cultural Revolution (1966-76). In 1964, a struggle over the future direction of mass music—fought along lines of musical genre—broke out among CCP cultural officials and critics responsible for overseeing musical production. In essence, the advocates of a new genre, called "modern revolutionary opera" (*geming xiandai xi*), triumphed over critics calling for the creation of a kind of "light music" (*qing yinyue*) that would allow for some degree of ideological relaxation in mass music.[25] This decision, stemming from the cultural priorities of the Yan'an forum, was symptomatic of the determination that music should serve not the leisure needs of individual people, but the political needs of an abstract entity, the people. By the late 1960's, as one recent Chinese commentator has observed, mass music had become restricted to "quotations songs" (*yulu ge*) which set the maxims of Mao Zedong to music, and "model music" (*yangban yinyue*) drawn from eight model revolutionary operas and their cinematic adaptations.[26]

Genre and Ideology in the Popular Music of the 'New Era'

My 70 year-old grandad's leading the nation
My sixty-year-old uncle's doing the four modernizations
My fifty-year-old uncle's strolling around
My forty-year-old brother's making sure his finances are sound
Some people are busy all day implementing reforms
Some people are busy trying to leave the country
Some people are busy gambling away their money
Some people are filling out unemployment forms[27]

The unprecedented degree of social change and cultural ferment of China's 'new era' (1978-1989) have been instrumental in spurring on a remarkable renaissance of Chinese popular music. Popular music, in turn, has come to play a vital role in the ideological and cultural struggles of this tumultuous period of rapid modernization. This resurgence was, of course, a

---

[25] Cheng Yun, 3-4. The proposal to institute "light music" was written by Li Ling in 1964 . It elicited a fierce attack printed in 1964 by *Renmin yinyue*, "Li Ling tongzhi de yinyue sixiang fanying le shenme wenti" [The problems reflected by Comrade Li Ling's thoughts on music] by Chen Ying, in which it was charged that in stressing music as leisure (*yinyue de yulexing*), Li had abandoned socialist principles.

[26] Zhang Jianguo and Kong Jun, "Shehui yinyue shenghuo sanyi" [Notes on the musical life of society], *Renmin yinyue*, 1989/11, 27.

[27] Chang Kuan, "Wanshi bugong" [Cynical], from *Chongxin jihua xianzai* [Making plans for now], EMI/ Dadi FH 500784, 1990. Chang Kuan is a rock singer from Beijing.

direct result of the sweeping program of economic reform and "opening to the outside world" instituted by Deng Xiaoping in 1978. Significantly, economic reforms, because they have demanded that music produced by the state be profitable not only politically but monetarily, have resulted in the loosening of the CCP's control of the ideological content of popular music. This loosening has resulted in renewed struggles over what kinds of ideologies popular music should convey to the Chinese people. For the first time since 1964, popular music's discursive horizons widened enough to allow some measure of real ideological contention. The music being produced by the state-run music industry became increasingly fragmented in terms of both style and content, and by 1986, an entirely new genre—rock music (*yaogun yinyue*)—began to constitute itself outside of these nationalized institutions and their (albeit widened) ideological constraints.

One of the first tangible benefits of the "open-door policy" was the widened availability of modern electrical appliances: radios, cassette players and television sets. New kinds of popular music followed rapidly on the heels of the importation of these technologies. From 1978 to 1980, China was flooded with imported cassettes and television programs. The popularity of Taiwanese singer Deng Lijun was representative of this early influx of popular music, and her impact on the development of popular music throughout the next decade cannot be underestimated. Her poetic, breathy ballads set the largely pentatonic melodic tradition of "yellow music" to electric guitars, drums, and swelling strings.[28] Audiences in the mainland were often overwhelmed with the novelty and expressive force of Deng Lijun's use of electrified instruments and modern recording techniques. As Jia Ding, one of the foremost songwriters in China, describes, her evocation of private emotional worlds that had heretofore been proscribed in mass music in favor of political themes was equally as revelatory:

> The first time I heard Deng Lijun's songs was in 1978. I just stood there listening for a whole afternoon. I never knew before that the world had such good music. I felt such pain. I cried. I was really very excited and touched, and suddenly realized that my work in the past had no emotional force.[29]

---

[28] Several of Deng's most popular songs are reworked versions of tunes dating from 1930's Shanghai, including the controversial "yellow" tune, "When Is He Coming Back Again" (*Heri jun zailai*).

[29] Han Xin'an and Andrew F. Jones, interview with Jia Ding, Beijing, July 5th, 1990.

By 1984, Chinese popular music had moved decisively in the direction of commodification and an ever greater reliance on the mass media. Imports of Hong Kong and Taiwanese cassettes and television series (from which many of the popular songs derived) grew steadily, while China began producing its own singers, songwriters, and cassettes, often following the Taiwanese and Hong Kong models in terms of musical style. Just as indigenous production of popular music began to control a greater share of the market, fundamental changes were occurring in the organization of the industry itself. As a result of economic reform, state-owned production units were being weaned from reliance on state subsidies and were delegated the responsibility of making profits. Inevitably, the monolithic dominance of ideological concerns began to be challenged by the imperatives of the market, and the industry was faced with the choice, as one official critic has put it, of either "serving the people" (*wei renmin fuwu*) or "serving the people's money" (*wei renminbi fuwu*).[30] The broadcast in 1984 of the "National Youth Singers Television Competition" (*Quanguo qingnian geshou dianshi dajiangsai*) and the ensuing institutionalization of the annual "New Year's Party" (*Chunjie wanhui*) program on Chinese Central Television (CCTV, *Zhongyang Dianshitai*) signalled the increasingly dominant role played by television in promoting and disseminating popular singers and songs.

In the seven years from 1984 to 1990, popular music in China continued to grow in significance and complexity. Popular music styles proliferated. Love songs based on Taiwanese and Hong Kong models (*shuqing gequ*) began to vie for popularity with disco (*disike*) and "energy songs" (*jinge*) that drew their inspiration from the mainstream popular music of Europe and North America. In 1988, the "Northwest Wind" (*xibeifeng*)—a style that fused the folk music of northwestern China with disco and rock rhythms—gained widespread popularity. Soon after, China's cassette market was flooded with another new style, "jail songs" (*qiuge*), that limited its lyrical scope to the laments of youthful convicts and the rusticated urban youth of the Cultural Revolution. Other musicians have attempted to incorporate jazz, blues, and western classical musics into this already chaotic mixture.[31] At the same time, a fundamentally different genre—spurred on by the efforts of small group of 'underground' musicians

---

[30] Editors of *Yinyue Yanjiu* , "Tan liuxing yinyue" [Discussing popular music], *Yinyue yanjiu*, 1988/2, 23.

[31] The songwriter, Wen Zhongjia, for instance, has used elements of jazz and country/western music in his arrangements of several "Northwest Wind" songs. The singer Liu Suola has made references to both Bach and the blues in her work.

in Beijing—began to develop outside of the realm of mainstream popular music: rock music.

Genre and Ideology

This somewhat confusing array of styles should not obscure the central fact that the construction of genre has become intimately related to the construction of cultural and political significance in Chinese popular music. For this reason, it is important to examine closely the critical discourse surrounding the issue of genre in Chinese popular music. Chinese notions of the essential nature of popular music usually do not differ from the 'working definition' presented above. The critic Miao Ye, writing in *People's Daily*, is in this respect typical:

> The term "popularized music" (*tongsu yinyue*), as is implied by its literal meaning, indicates music that is commensurate with the level and needs of the masses, and which is easily absorbed and accepted by the masses. This category can be very broad, including ancient, modern, Chinese, foreign, national and folk musics that are expressly produced to be easily comprehensible. Even so, the type of "popularized music" I will discuss here is music that lays stress on an aesthetic of pleasure, that expresses the daily life of society as its primary content, and whose creative form is based upon the rhythms of the world's modern dance musics. This latter type of music is also generally termed "popular music" (*liuxing yinyue*). In today's society, popular music is an artistic commodity that circulates in the market in great quantity, and with rapid turnover.[32]

Miao Ye's definition is particularly valuable for the light it throws on recent critical debates over the terminological distinction between "popular music" (*liuxing yinyue*) and "popularized music" (*tongsu yinyue*). The latter term was already in use by the 1920's to describe leftist film music and 'yellow music.' The former, however, is a relatively new term. Jin Zhaojun, the popular music editor for *Renmin Yinyue* (*People's Music*), claims that "*tongsu yinyue*" was coined in 1984 by an "old comrade" who

---

[32] Miao Ye, "Zai kaifang de chaoliu zhong qiu fazhan: dui woguo tongsu yinyue chuangzuo wenti de sikao" [Seeking development in the midst of opening up to the outside world: thoughts on the question of artistic production in China's popular music], *Renmin ribao*, January 5, 1988. Unless otherwise noted, all translations from Chinese are my own.

disliked the associations to "yellow music" conjured up by the word "*liuxing yinyue*." *Tongsu* music is essentially a 'politically correct' euphemism, and its use is often linked to shifts in the political climate. In the wake of the "counter-revolutionary turmoil" of June 4, 1989, for instance, the use of "*tongsu yinyue*" in published articles noticeably increased, while "*liuxing yinyue*" fell into disuse.[33]

Perhaps because of the predication of musical terminology on rapidly shifting ideological (and sometimes sociological) considerations, Chinese and Western critics alike have come to view the taxonomization of various Chinese musical genres as "inherently problematic."[34] Since 1949, folk songs (*minjian gequ*), Chinese opera, Chinese and European classical musics, and revolutionary mass music have all been disseminated through the mass media. Clearly, each of these forms can be seen as *tongsu yinyue*. In terms of musical style and lyrical content, however, none of them can be strictly defined as *liuxing yinyue*.[35] While the "Northwest Wind," disco, and love songs modelled on the popular music of Hong Kong and Taiwan may be subsumed by the larger category of *tongsu yinyue*, their musical and lyrical content (as well as their saturation of the marketplace) are more aptly described by the term *liuxing yinyue*. Unfortunately, debates on the complexities of categorization continue unabated, and taxonomies like that posited by Miao Ye have by no means forged critical concensus. Instead, Chinese scholarship on popular music remains plagued by "conceptual chaos and theoretical weakness."[36]

In terms of everyday usage, popular songs that would be indistinguishable from folk songs (*minge*) without the accompaniment of electrified instruments and that cater to a middle-aged audience are generally referred to as *tongsu*, while music that has absorbed Western popular harmonies, and appeals to predominantly youthful audiences are called *liuxing*.[37] Popular music imported from Hong Kong, Taiwan, and the West is also referred to as *liuxing* music. The category of *liuxing* music is further subdivided into a variety of different musical styles (*fengge*), including "Northwest Wind," "jail songs," Hong Kong/Taiwan love songs,

---

[33] Interview with Jin Zhaojun, Beijing, June 20, 1990.
[34] Manuel, 221.
[35] One interviewee, the songwriter Li Lifu, disagreed with this point, claiming that "popular music is just popular music" ("*liuxing jiushi liuxing*"), i.e. style is irrelevant so long as the music reaches a mass audience. Han and Jones, interview with Li Lifu, Beijing, June 29, 1990.
[36] Editors of *Yinyue yanjiu*, 17.
[37] I am indebted to Jin Zhaojun for this schematization.

and disco. Each of these *liuxing* styles (as well as "popularized" renditions of folk songs and opera), though, are also commonly encompassed by the term *tongsu yinyue*.

These categorizations are subtly informed by ideological considerations, for *tongsu* clearly implies political legitimacy and ideological orthodoxy, while *liuxing* continues to connote 'yellow music,' westernization, and heterodox activity.[38] Significantly, neither critics nor musicians are willing to situate *rock music* in any one of these categories, preferring instead to view it as a separate generic entity despite its clear affinities with *liuxing yinyue*. In interviews, popular singers and songwriters often discussed the utilization of the techniques of rock music in *tongsu* music, but without exception persisted in identifying rock music *per se* as a separate genre. Rock musicians tended to lump all other popular music together under the rubric of *tongsu yinyue*, and proceeded to situate themselves outside of this grouping. In both cases, this exclusion was invariably made on the grounds of the utterly distinctive quality of the *ideology* that surrounds Chinese rock music.[39]

In short, genre is a function of ideology, not musical style. Moreover, interviewees indicated that in China today there are two contending genres: *tongsu* music and rock music, each of which, in turn, encompass a number of different musical *styles*. For the remainder of the paper, *tongsu* music will denote the products, institutions, ideologies and practices of the nationalized popular music industry. Rock music will be used to denote a separate generic entity, characterized by its exclusion from the institutions and practices of *tongsu* music, and its oppositional ideological stance.

Ideology, of course, is a difficult term to pin down, but it is central to understanding the divergent ways in which *tongsu* music and rock music in China function as vehicles for the articulation of cultural and political struggle. In its most literal sense, ideology indicates the set of beliefs, symbols, and doctrines held by any given group in reference to their cultural, social, and political life. This is the specific sense in which I will use the terms "political" and/or "cultural ideology" throughout the book. As I elaborate in the second chapter, these ideologies are neither monolithic, static nor uncontested; instead they are the instrumental means through

---

[38] Interview with Jin Zhaojun.

[39] The claim that rock music constitutes a completely separate ideology (*yishi*) was made without exception by every interviewee.

which various social groupings empower themselves, contend for power, or struggle to retain power.

In describing the divergent ways in which popular music genres construct and convey cultural and political ideology, interviewees almost invariably characterized *tongsu* music and rock music in terms of their "*yishi*," or sensibility. "*Yishi*" literally means "consciousness", but connotes the far wider realm of sensibilities, and the way in which they are articulated through activity. The term is often used to describe literary movements (as in "roots-seeking sensibility," "*xungen yishi*"), political attitudes (as in "democratic consciousness," "*minzhu yishi*"), and cultural trends (as in"cultural nostalgia," "*huigui yishi*"). These varied sensibilities, in turn, are seen as the building blocks of specific cultural and political ideologies: in Chinese, "ideology" is simply "*yishi*" coupled with patterning and form (*yishi xingtai*).

If the categorization of different genres in Chinese popular music is a function of sensibility, then it becomes essential to examine the contexts in which these sensibilities are manifested in activity. For it is only through the concrete activities of musicians, audiences, and critics within a socio-cultural frame that generic sensibilities are given form as cultural and political ideology.

The first of these contexts is production. Who composes the music? Who writes the lyrics? Who plays the music? How do the socio-economic positions and institutional affiliations of the musicians and songwriters inform their sensibilities? Who provides the recording facilities and manufacturing equipment? Who pays for these facilities? Who controls the content of the music?

The second is dissemination. Does the music reach its audiences through television, films, radio, and cassettes, or through some other medium? How does mass media dissemination affect the way in which it is perceived by its audiences? Who decides what can and cannot be distributed through the mass media? Performances, of course, are another important context for the dissemination of popular music. Where is the music performed? Who organizes the performances? Who owns the venue? What kind of people make up the audience? How do all these factors shape the way the musicians play, and the way the audience responds?

The musicians' own creative activities are a third vitally important context. How do the sensibilities, and perceptions of their societal role and occupational affiliation shape the final musical text? How significant is authorial intent—the creative, social, and political aims of the singer or songwriter—to the way in which music is received by its audiences? A final, and closely related, context is the critical discourse surrounding the music. How does what is said and written about popular music affect the musicians' conceptions of their work? Does it affect the behavior and perceptions of the listener or the concert-goer?

Within the limited scope of this study, I do not claim to answer all of these questions with any kind of finality. Nor do I contend that the meaning of the music is solely determined by these contexts. Signification in popular music is mercurial by nature; its meanings are ultimately created through the complex interplay of all the activities noted above, and the way in which audiences enjoy, re- or mis-interpret, and *use* the music in the course of leisure, work, or political activity.[40]

Tongsu Music and Rock Music

In each of the contextual realms I have proposed above, there exist fundamental differences between *tongsu* music and rock. The production of *tongsu* music is sanctioned, supported, and controlled by the CCP. Its performers, musicians, composers, and technicians are employed by a network of nationalized song and dance troupes (*gewutuan*) and audio-visual publishers. Songs are written by professional songwriters to be sung by professional singers accompanied by musicians affiliated with the *gewutuan*. There are no independent music groups (*yuedui*) outside of the *gewutuan*; and audience attention is thus focused entirely on individual singers. Some singers and musicians, however, do work on a free-lance basis for these state-owned production units. Others have become private entrepreneurs (*getihu*) who band together with a manager to sell their musical services by touring the nation and performing on a contractual basis for local, state-owned cultural organizations. This practice, colloquially referred to as "going to the cave" (*zouxue*), has become increasingly common in the past few years.[41]

---

[40] This is one of the most salient points raised in Simon Frith's introduction to the sociology of popular music, *Sound Effects: Youth, Leisure, and the Politics of Rock 'n' Roll*, (New York: Pantheon Books, 1981).

[41] See Zhu Xingyi, Ge Guang, Qiao Guoliang, "Zou xue! Zou xue!" [Going to the cave! Going to the cave!] in *Shehui wenti chensi lu: baogao wenxue xuan* [Serious considerations of social problems: an anthology of literary reportage], (Beijing: Renmin wenxue chubanshe, 1990), 216-250.

Rock music, however, is essentially an unofficial, underground phenomena. It is actively disapproved of, and often restricted by, the CCP. Its musicians are 'unemployed' amateurs, with no affiliation with any nationalized work unit (*danwei*). Instead, musicians join together in rock bands (*yaogun yuedui*)—thirty of which were estimated by one journalist to be active in Beijing as of June, 1990.[42] Financial support for the music derives either from the musicians' own resources, or from foreign investors. In marked contrast to *tongsu* music, rock musicians write and perform their own songs. This fact itself was often cited in interviews as a key element of the rock sensibility.[43]

The manner in which the two genres reach their audiences is also fundamentally different. *Tongsu* is disseminated nationwide through the mass media: television, radio, and cassettes. Rock music is seldom, if ever, broadcast on the radio, and as of July 1991, only two rock albums—Cui Jian's *New Long March Rock* (*Xin changzheng lushang de yaogun*) and *Solution* (*Jiejue*)—have been distributed nationwide.[44] Rock music is effectively barred from appearing on the most influential (and thus most strictly regulated) of these media, television. Popular music concerts are held in large state-operated auditoriums and theaters. Rock shows take place almost exclusively in privately run bars and restaurants, and less frequently in college cafeterias, and parks.[45] Often these venues are either owned or operated by foreigners, and foreigners usually constitute a portion of the audience.

In terms of musical content, *tongsu* music is quite varied. Stylistic categorization is usually cast either in terms of the way in which any given piece is sung (*changfa*), or on the basis of melodic or rhythmic factors. Singing styles range from the "lyrical" (*shuqing*, often in the 'feminine,' crooning style popularized by Deng Lijun) to the "energetic" or "hard" (*jinge, ying*, usually a 'masculine,' rough tone associated with the

---

[42] Tong Wei, "Rock 'n' Roll China," *Nexus: China in Focus*, (Summer 1990), 17.

[43] Interview with Jin Zhaojun, and Han and Jones, interview with Jing Gangshan, Beijing, July 2, 1990.

[44] Cui Jian's *Xin changzheng lushang de yaogun* was released by a state-run unit, Zhongguo luyou shengxiang chubanshe [China Tourism Audio-visual Publishers] in March, 1989. The record's release came about only through the intervention of foreign investors. The release in 1991 of *Jiejue* by *Zhongguo Beiguang Shengxiang Gongsi* [China Northern Lights Audio-Visual Company] was delayed for almost a year by CCP officials. The lyrics for two of the more politically sensitive songs included in the collection are conspicuously absent from the liner notes.

[45] Again, Cui Jian is the exception to this rule. His large-scale concerts are discussed in depth in chapter five.

"Northwest Wind").[46] Melodically, songs can be classified by their degree of reliance upon pentatonic scales (which remain extremely common). A style like the "Northwest Wind," for instance, draws heavily on melodic material taken from a larger melodic tradition of "northern tunes" (*beifang diaozi*). More Westernized popular songs (*liuxing gequ*) often use melodies that would not be out of place on American Top 40 radio. Disco, of course, is notable not for its melodic content but its emphasis on a driving, often synthesized rhythm section. Generally speaking, *tongsu* music, regardless of stylistic affinity, lays more stress on melodic than rhythmic content. The influence of both "yellow music" syncretism and the tradition of Nie Er and Xian Xinghai (i.e. marches, orchestral flourishes, and certain verse forms based on "revolutionary songs") are all readily discernible.

Rock musicians have abandoned both "yellow music" and revolutionary song. Chinese rock is directly modelled upon its Anglo-American counterpart. The kinds of stylistic differences within the genre reflect this fact. Bands like Breathing (*Huxi yuedui*), Tang Dynasty (*Tangchao yuedui*), and Black Panthers (*Heibao yuedui*) play heavy metal (*zhong jinshu*), while bands like Tutu (*Tutu yuedui*) and a singer like He Yong are self-styled "punks" (*benke*).[47] Pentatonic melodies are extremely rare; melodic lines are often de-emphasized in favor of short, repeated riff-like phrases. Vocal tone is almost invariably throaty and rough. Electric guitars (often distorted) and standard 4/4 rock rhythms dominate the sound. Occasionally, a song will feature a reggae or ska beat.[48]

For reasons that I set out in more detail in the next chapter, lyrics are perhaps the most explicit indicator of the ideological content of *tongsu* songs. As the songwriter Li Lifu has explained, *tongsu* song lyrics can be divided into three broad categories: propaganda songs, songs that express the personal feelings of the songwriter, and songs through which the songwriter seeks to exert influence over his audiences by promoting "certain ideological

---

[46] Han and Jones, interview with Jing Gangshan. Examples of "lyrical" singers currently popular are Zhao Li and Cai Guoqing. Examples of "hard" singers are Jing Gangshan and Sun Guoqing.

[47] "Black Panthers" is not a reference to Black nationalism, or the American political party of the same name.

[48] Examples of this kind are Cui Jian's "Congtou zailai" [From the start again] and Tutu Band's "Shenme ye juebuchu" [Can't find any feeling]. Ska and reggae derive from the popular music of Jamaica. Instead of stressing the second and fourth beats of each measure, reggae and ska place their downbeats on the first and third beat. The presence of these Caribbean rhythms in Chinese rock is a direct result of the influence of a Madagascaran musician who played lead guitar for Cui Jian's ADO band. The continued popularity of the form is testified by the recent release in Hong Kong of an album called *Beijing Reggae*, in which three members of the ADO Band and an American producer (Jeffrey Cheen) present a number of Chinese *tongsu* and folk tunes set to a reggae beat.

trends"; i.e. trends that may or may not be ideologically orthodox in the eyes of the CCP.[49] In practice, *tongsu* song lyrics are often exhortatory, patriotic, or explicitly linked to prevailing political slogans. The second category mentioned by Li Lifu includes love songs, or songs with personal, philosophical content. The third category is for our purposes, the most interesting, for it is in this arena that the articulation of contending political and cultural ideologies most frequently takes place. This phenomena, as I discuss in depth in the second chapter, has been especially common in the songs of the "Northwest Wind," which played a prominent role in popularizing the controversial reflections on the nature of Chinese culture and identity that pervade 'new era' literary and intellectual culture.

Finally, *tongsu* song lyrics tend to take as their object not the individual, but the collective emotional and political life of the nation. Their use of language is often relatively formal and poetic; set phrases drawn from China's literary and folk traditions (*chengyu*) abound. With the advent of the "Northwest Wind," the use of rural dialects to evoke a 'folksy' feeling has also become common.

The stated aim of rock lyricists is itself intimately linked to rock's most distinctive ideological stance: the direct, authentic expression of inner emotion and individualism in the face of an oppressive, feudalistic society. As I will explore later in some detail, this lyrical stance often takes on a curiously dual function. Songs of the individual serve as covert political and cultural ideology; the discourse of individual authenticity becomes a kind of linguistic marker through which the rock music subculture forges itself as a subcultural community, and directs its message to the larger society within which it is embedded. While overt political themes rarely figure in their lyrics (in contrast to their *tongsu* counterparts), many songs are quite clearly intended to address cultural and political issues. Love songs are extremely rare; when they do appear, their lyrics tend towards a kind of idiosyncratic ambiguity that lends itself to allegorical readings.[50] The language employed by rock singers is urban, colloquial, and contemporary. When poetic imagery is employed, it usually harks back not to folkloric or traditional literary sources, but the works of the experimental and intensely individualistic "Misty" poets (*menglongshi*).[51]

---

[49] Han and Jones, interview with Li Lifu.

[50] I discuss one such song, Cui Jian's "Yikuai hongbu" [A piece of red cloth] in detail in chapter five.

[51] The epithet derives from the ostensible "obscurity" and modernism of their works. "Misty" poetry was perhaps the most influential school of poetry in the 1980's. The movement arose

The self-perceptions and aspirations of the musicians themselves—as derived from the series of interviews I conducted in the Summer of 1990 in Beijing—are another context through which we may understand the varying ways in which these genres produce meaning. In the case of *tongsu* music, there exists a fundamental division between songwriters and singers. Ultimately, songwriters are among the most powerful figures in the state-owned popular music industry, for they exercise enormous power over what gets sung, how it is sung, and who sings it. They maintain close ties with editors and operatives within the record, television, radio, and concert promotion industries, as well as with the CCP cadres responsible for overseeing these endeavors. Interviewees as a group tended to be middle-aged, well-educated, articulate, and satisfied with their occupation. They often expressed either skepticism or disdain towards rock musicians.[52] Interviews with *tongsu* singers, on the other hand, revealed an altogether different tableau. Singers felt themselves to be at the mercy of songwriters, CCP officials connected with the mass media, as well as their work units. Singers are unable to write or perform their own compositions, or even to choose which songs to sing. As a result, they avowed that *tongsu* singers as a group have no common aims or ideals save financial success. This sense of helplessness and frustration was often focused upon the institution of televised singing contests upon which Chinese pop stars depend for promotion, and expressed in terms of emotional and physical violation.[53] They were consistently sympathetic to rock music and rock musicians.

Rock musicians inhabit an entirely different milieu. Often, they have left careers as *tongsu* musicians (or in one case, as a television anchorwoman) expressly in order to play rock music. They write and perform their own music, are unaffiliated with any work unit, and have no working relationships with either *tongsu* songwriters or the official media. They inhabit a tightly-knit social circle composed of other rock musicians, and rock devotees, and perform at collective rock "parties" (the English word is usually used) where up to five bands are featured. Interviews revealed a coherent and commonly held oppositional ideology of anti-feudalism, individualism, and authentic expression, and a conviction that playing rock music was less a vocation than a mission. Finally, and perhaps

out of the underground press formed in 1979 by participants in the "Democracy Wall" movement. Many of its leading exponents (Bei Dao, Gu Cheng, Duo Duo) have been forced into exile in the aftermath of the 1989 democracy movement.

[52] Han and Jones, interviews with Li Lifu, Jia Ding, San Bao, and Wen Zhongjia, June-July, 1990.

[53] These statements are based on interviews with the *tongsu* singers An Dong, Hu Yue, Jing Gangshan, Liu Huan, Wo Peng and Zhao Li in Beijing, June-July, 1990.

unsurprisingly, they situated themselves in opposition to *tongsu* music, and frequently made reference to its superficiality and vacuity.[54]

The final contextual frame to which I will refer to throughout the book is the critical discourse that surrounds, and to some extent helps to shape, the way in which the music is received by its audiences. In a sense, this is the realm that is most overtly connected to the issues of political and cultural ideology. Chinese critics and scholars are far more interested in social prescription than theoretical description; their "musicology is inseparable from sociology."[55] Popular music is defined almost entirely in terms of social cause and effect. Official critics routinely extol the the usefulness of popular music as an important tool in the construction of a "modern socialist spiritual civilization."[56] Popular music's negative social consequences, however, are potentially dire indeed:

> In the Western countries rock music has never been played from the stage of the music hall, but in China we put similar things on stages meant for serious music and treat them as art. What confusion! Every single person with a social conscience should rise up against this [musical] opium that damages art, damages our national culture, and damages the entire Chinese national spirit.[57]

While this sort of polemic is relatively unusual, it is representative of the high moral seriousness with which popular music is viewed by Chinese critics. These critics share a recognition of the enormous power of music either to consolidate or undermine the social order. The contention that music both shapes and reflects the nature of popular consciousness permeates China's musicological and popular journals. Jin Zhaojun's explication of the huge popularity of the "Northwest Wind" in popular music is symptomatic of this critical emphasis:

> ...internal changes in musical style are due not to isolated trends in music, but to socio-psychological demands determined by the life of a society.[58]

---

[54] These statements are based on interviews with the rock musicians Cui Jian, Dong Dong, Gao Qi, Liu Xiaosong, and Zhu Xiaomin in Beijing, June-July, 1990.

[55] Cheng Yun, 2. Jin Zhaojun strongly affirmed the validity of this statement.

[56] Li Tianyi, "Tongsu yinyue heyuan luoru digu" [What caused *tongsu* music's decline?], *Renmin yinyue*, 1989/11, 27.

[57] Editors of *Yinyue yanjiu*, 21.

[58] Jin Zhaojun, "Feng cong nali lai: ping getan xibei feng" [Where's the wind coming from: an appraisal of popular music's 'Northwest Wind'], *Renmin ribao*, August 23, 1988, 5.

This vision of the intertwinement of music and society is more than a little reminiscent of the commonplaces of Confucian musical exegesis.[59] Chinese Marxism and the Confucian tradition share a common interest in "reconciling the spontaneous expression of feeling [in music] and its normative regulation," in harnessing music's more dangerous pleasures to the service of the social order.[60] As I will explore later, the debates that have raged around the social implications of popular music and rock since its reintroduction to mainland China in 1978 cannot be fully understood in isolation from this ideologically charged critical context. In contemporary China, pop songs are not merely pop songs; in tune with the critical spirit of Confucian texts like the *Record of Music* (*Yue ji*), they are often seen as complex indices of the tenor of the times:

> The tones of a well-managed age are at rest and happy, its government is balanced. The tones of an age of turmoil are bitter and full of anger: its government is perverse. The tones of a ruined state are filled with lament and brooding: its people are in difficulty.[61]

Interestingly, popular music criticism itself has often served as an accurate barometer of the cultural and political struggles of the 'new era'. Critics as well as songwriters may seek to "guide a certain type of intellectual trend"; their critiques are also disseminated through a mass medium, print.

"A Superfluous Story": *Tongsu*, Rock, and Cultural Struggle

Fiction and poetry have also played a role in shaping and reflecting the nature of popular music in the 'new era.'[62] Liu Suola's "A Superfluous Story," written by an author who is herself a popular singer, provides us with an insightful window into the issues of genre and ideology which I have introduced in this chapter. Moreover, the story's portrayal of the life and emotional world of a young popular musician, Xiao Hu, prefigures

---

[59] For a longer discussion of the affinities between Marxist-Leninist and Confucian notions of the role of music in society see Arnold Perris, "Music as Propaganda: Art at the Command of Doctrine in the People's Republic of China," *Ethnomusicology* 17/1 (1983).

[60] Stephen Owen, trans., "Selections from the *Record of Music*." Unpublished manuscript, 86.

[61] Ibid., 88.

[62] For another fictional account of the intertwinement of youth culture and popular music, see Liu Yiran, "Yaogun qingnian" [Rock and roll youth], *Qingnian wenxue*, 1988/10, 4-28. A translation of the story is included in Geremie Barmé and Linda Jaivin, eds., *New Ghosts, Old Dreams: Chinese Rebel Voices*, (New York: Times Books, 1992), 5-22.

many of the issues and themes I explore in detail in the following chapters of this study. In detailing the wranglings over the lyrical content of one song between Xiao Hu and the Propaganda Chief of her work unit, "A Superfluous Story" affords us an 'inside' view of the process of popular music production. This process, as Liu makes clear, is in every sense a struggle—one in which many of the cultural and political dilemmas of 'new era' culture figure prominently. At the same time, the story serves to remind us that these larger struggles take place on the level of the individual and her aspirations and frustrations. Xiao Hu's sense of violation at the hands of the the Propaganda Chief and the media echo those of the *tongsu* singers I profile in chapter three; her search for moral self-definition in an absurd and hypocritical social milieu is an early and eloquent articulation of the rebelliousness that continues to inform the ideology of China's emergent rock music subculture that I investigate in chapters four and five.

"A Superfluous Story," first published in February 1986, was itself a direct response to the Anti-Spiritual Pollution Campaign of 1983-4, during which the CCP attempted to stem the tide of anti-socialist "bourgeois liberalization" and westernization in the arts. Popular music was among the CCP's principal targets in the campaign. In October 1983, the People's Music Publishing House (*Renmin yinyue chubanshe*) issued a harsh attack on popular music entitled, "How to Recognize Pornographic Music."[63] The music of Liu Suola (among others) was attacked for its "individualism," and the production of one of her cassette recordings was halted.[64] These events, although only obliquely referred to in the text, form an important backdrop for understanding the rhetorical goals of Liu's intricate narrative.[65]

In "A Superfluous Story," the power of popular music to transform individual psychology is direct and undeniable. The story begins with a long monologue in which Xiao Hu ponders her crisis of moral self-definition:

---

[63] Bai Jieming, "Yaogun fanshen le?" ("Has Rock Stood Up?"), *Jiushi niandai*, 1988/11, 94.

[64] Patricia Libretti, "Shouting from the Mountaintops," *China Now* /130, 35.

[65] The clearest reference to the Anti-Spiritual Pollution Campaign is part of Xiao Hu's long initial monologue, "Beijing has a psychological counseling center, but I still haven't heard if there are psychiatrists -- not those doctors they have now in the psychiatric ward of the major hospitals, but those psychiatrists who treat the patients who aren't sick." The passage becomes more transparent when we realize that "mental illness" in Chinese is literally a "spiritual sickness" (*jingshenbing*). Liu Suola, "Duoyu de Gushi" [A Superfluous Story], *Shouhuo*, 1986/2, 111.

Perhaps it was rock music that made me muddle-headed, that made me forget the correct rhythms of life, forget normal ideology, and how to express my own thoughts normally. I couldn't listen to it anymore, nor could I stop listening; when I didn't listen I couldn't even express myself at all, and when I did listen not being able to express myself didn't matter anyway.[66]

Xiao Hu resolves to reconcile herself to "normal ideology" as part of a larger effort to discover a moral standard by which she can live:

I want to quietly study in my free time how certain people can think about things that way, how they can stretch a matter as big as a sesame seed into a noodle several miles long, how they can see a good person as a convicted murderer, how they can turn a kiss into the decline of the empire...[67]

This search is structured around her desire for a "measuring stick" with which she can satisfy her passionate concern for moral authenticity and the truthful expression of her thoughts and feelings.

It rapidly becomes clear, however, that the world of "normal ideology" is riddled with absurdity and falsification. The Propaganda Chief of the factory where Xiao Hu works is not only the final arbiter of popular music content, but Liu's most potent symbol of all that is wrong with "normal ideology." He is a political opportunist who has bent every passing political campaign to his own advantage. He derides the band's members for looking like "foreign trash," but wears a bathrobe to work so that he can show off its foreign label. He writes an article praising Xiao Hu's band, and later changes his pen-name in order to write an article condemning them. This attack is followed by an article in his own name attacking the condemnation, on the heels of which he writes a final article refuting the attack on the condemnation of the original positive review. For this "visionary" promotional work, the Chief reaps rich financial awards from the local print and television industry, suggesting that the effort to serve both the "people" and the "people's money" can indeed be combined in a uniquely corrupt fashion.

---

[66] Ibid., 110.
[67] Ibid., 110.

Early on in the story, Xiao Hu is enlisted by the Propaganda Chief to write a new song:

> "Xiao Hu, I'm Secretary Wang. I've been looking all over for you. Where have you been hiding?"
>
> "I go to work everyday."
>
> "Really? I have some good news for you. According to our Propaganda Chief, your group is getting hotter and hotter! The TV station also wants to film a clip of your band. Are you happy?"
>
> "Really?"
>
> "Right now the propaganda team wants you to write a song immediately that will represent young people. Your band has to sing it, and all the young people in the factory have to sing it. We're turning this responsibility over to you."[68]

Clearly, the song is not so much to be created, as engineered to the specifications of the Propaganda Chief and the media with which he maintains close connections. Xiao Hu is forced to write and rewrite the song three times; each re-writing represents in a very real sense a struggle over political ideology, over the issue of who will define, and thus control, whom:

> "'Kissing', 'losing sleep'—these lyrics don't describe contemporary youth...Then there's the end of the song. It should be the people, not 'ourselves.'"
>
> "Aren't we the people? Aren't the people us?"
>
> "No, the people are the people, the people are the *People*. They're not me, and not you, they're not anyone, they're the people.
>
> "Then who would that be?"
>
> "The people."[69]

Xiao Hu revises the lyrics on the spot, disingenuously substituting "What was it that made us.dream all our dreams/ It was us ourselves" with "What was it that made us dream what we should have dreamed?/ It was the

---

[68] Ibid., 111-2.

[69] Ibid., 113.

people, that's just the p-e-o-p-l-e." As the meeting concludes, the Propaganda Chief unsuccessfully attempts to seduce Xiao Hu.

In the course of their third interview, the Propaganda Chief informs Xiao Hu that even these lyrics don't pass muster. He goes on to reveal his contempt for the 'superfluous' young workers of the factory, likening them to "extra eggs." This triggers in Xiao Hu a realization of the very real power he wields over her and her generation:

> But the Chief in actual fact was more important than us—after all was said and done, he had a foreign bathrobe, and he could wear it to work. If I dared to wear a bathrobe to work, the foreman would throw me right into the gears of the machines.[70]

At this point, the Chief pinches her hand, his eyes "gleaming with the very image of obscenity." Xiao Hu has found her measuring stick. She re-writes the song once more in the form of a ringing condemnation of everything the Chief and his "normal ideology" stand for:

> ...What made you lose your youth and at the same time not be able to stand seeing other people's youth?
>
> What made you lose your purity and at the same time begrudge other people's purity?
>
> What made you unable to lose your purity and at the same time helplessly resent that others have lost theirs?
>
> ...What made you talk about everything under the sun without getting through to other people, fooling yourself, fooling other people, still thinking you're the man who's lived through it all?
>
> What did you pass through to live? What have you lived through? What have you lived? Have you lived?
>
> In that world of yours without heaven, without earth, without sobs, without smiles, without songs, without love, without yells, without curses, without him, without me, without this,

---

[70] Ibid., 115.

without that, it doesn't matter if it's the first or the seventh egg that the chicken laid—they're all rotten eggs.[71]

Xiao Hu gives up her privileged position at the factory as a singer, resolves to smash her television set, and returns to the factory floor.

What "A Superfluous Story" reveals most clearly is that the stakes of ideological struggle in popular music are very high. Popular songs can be a vehicle for both empowerment (as with Xiao Hu's final liberating gesture), or the retention of power. These battles within popular music are fought over a complex of social dilemmas that have pervaded 'new era' culture. What sort of modernity is China marching towards? Will Deng Xiaoping's "Four Modernizations" (of industry, agriculture, education, and the military) be extended to include what the dissident Wei Jingsheng has called the "Fifth Modernization": political democratization? To what extent is individual liberty permissible, or even possible, in light of what is perceived as China's 'feudal' and authoritarian cultural legacy? Need modernization entail complete Westernization? These battles, in turn, are often fought across generational lines. In particular, the development of rock music has paralleled the growth of the burgeoning urban youth culture from which "A Superfluous Story" clearly draws its concerns.

Moreover, many of the situations and ideological stances portrayed in "A Superfluous Story" are uncannily reminiscent of those described to me by interviewees. *Tongsu* songwriters are compelled engineer songs to serve the "People" the Propaganda Chief so eloquently characterizes. These efforts at ideological control are usually carried out at the level of lyrical content. *Tongsu* singers consistently express a feeling of victimization at the hands of their work units and the media, often in terms of physical violation. Finally, Xiao Hu's sensibility—in its insistence on an authenticity rendered inevitably confrontational by the nature of the surrounding socio-cultural milieu—is an almost perfect blueprint of the attitudes and aims of participants in Beijing's rock music subculture.

It is important to bear in mind, though, that "A Superfluous Story" is to some extent a caricature, however useful it may be in mapping for us the terms of struggle in popular music. As I will detail in the following chapter, the process of struggle is rarely one-sided. The rock sensibility is not purely oppositional; *tongsu* music is not simply a tool of hegemonic discourse. Instead, meaning in popular music is made, and

---

[71] Ibid., 116.

contested, throughout the course of its production, dissemination, and reception by audiences.

2

IDEOLOGICAL STRUGGLE IN *TONGSU* MUSIC

In this chapter, I analyze the ways in which cultural and political ideologies are conveyed through *tongsu* music. If *tongsu* music is indeed a site for the creation and dissemination of contending ideologies in contemporary China, then it is important to locate the specific spheres in which these processes occur. I begin by hammering out a notion of just what constitutes the public sphere in contemporary China, and continue on to an exploration of the involvement of popular music in the private, quotidian realm of individual emotion and desire. I then discuss the interaction of these two realms in the context of both the ideological functions of popular music in contemporary China, and ongoing critiques of mass culture in the West. Finally, drawing on recent Western analyses of the ways in which audiences respond to mass cultural products, I explore the ideological content of *tongsu* music in terms of how it both propagates the hegemony of the CCP, and serves as negotiated arena in which many of the ideological struggles of 'new era' China are played out.

Tongsu Music in the Public Sphere

Tongsu music, because its dissemination is carried out by the mass media, cannot help but to participate in the public sphere. This participation in the public sphere is fundamental to its role in the articulation of cultural and political ideologies. The notion of the public sphere as a distinct social entity originates from the work of Jürgen Habermas, a German social thinker loosely affiliated with the Frankfurt School of critical theory.[1] In Habermas' conception, the public sphere arose in 17th and 18th century bourgeois European society as a realm independent of both state authority and the concerns of the market. Ideally, the public sphere would serve as:

---

[1] See Jürgen Habermas, *The Structural Transformation of the Public Sphere: An Inquiry into a Category of Bourgeois Society*, (Cambridge, MA: The MIT Press, 1989).

...a theater in modern societies in which political participation is enacted through the medium of talk. It is the space in which citizens deliberate about their common affairs, hence, an institutionalized arena of discursive interaction. This arena is conceptually distinct from the state; it is a site for the production and circulation of discourses that can in principle be critical of the state.[2]

Habermas goes on to narrate the usurpation of this public sphere in the industrialized nations of the twentieth century by the expansion of state power and the mass media. The media becomes a kind of public sphere, but one in which rational discourse is irretrievably compromised by its imbrication with both state power and the dominant ideologies of capitalism. Publicity becomes less an impartial indicator of bourgeois public opinion than a coercive tool for the maintenance of social, cultural, and political dominance.

A similar historical process could be said to have taken place in twentieth century China. A nascent public sphere, created by the growth of the press, provincial congresses, and merchants' and native place (*tongxianghui*) organizations in the late Imperial and Republican periods, was shattered by the CCP in the years following 1949.[3] Rational discourse was replaced by Maoist propaganda. State power brooked no criticism in its relentless drive to control every aspect of both the public sphere and private life. This drive, in turn, was largely effected through the agency of the state-controlled mass media.

Recent critical efforts to revive and revise Habermas' public sphere have been forced to come to terms with Habermas' negative assessment of the mass media.[4] The reason for this critical quandary is clear; the mass media are perhaps the single most pervasive "institutionalized arena of discursive interaction" in a range of contemporary societies, including China. I propose that in 'new era' China the mass media does indeed constitute a *limited* public sphere. While inextricably penetrated by state

---

[2] Nancy Fraser, "Rethinking the Public Sphere," *Social Text*, 25/26 (Winter 1990), 57.

[3] Mary Rankin, lecture on "The Origins of a Chinese Public Sphere: Local Elites and Community Affairs in Late Imperial China," New England China Seminar, Harvard University, November 27, 1990. Also see Andrew Nathan and Leo Ou-fan Lee, "The Beginnings of Mass Culture: Journalism and Fiction in the Late Ch'ing," in David Johnson, et al., eds., *Popular Culture in Late Imperial China,* (Berkeley: University of California Press, 1985), 360-395.

[4] See for instance, Dana Polan, "The Public's Fear, or Media as Monster in Habermas, Negt, and Kluge," *Social Text*: 25/26 (1990), 260-6.

power, the mass media remains the most significant public forum in which issues of common concern are discussed and debated on a national level.

It is important to remember that this public sphere operates only in the context of the cultural hegemony of the CCP. The concept of cultural hegemony, derived from the work of Antonio Gramsci, can be roughly defined as an ideological construct which:

> ...defines within its terms the mental horizon, the universe of possible meanings, of a whole sector of relations in a society or culture; and...carries with it the stamp of legitimacy—it appears coterminous with what is 'natural,' or 'taken for granted' about the social order."[5]

In China, the "universe of possible meanings" conveyed by the mass media are circumscribed by the political dominance of the CCP. On a basic level, the mass media in China is constrained by what the Central Committee of the CCP has called the "Four Cardinal Principles" in the realm of ideology. They are "adherence to the socialist road, adherence to the dictatorship of the proletariat, adherence to the leadership of the Communist Party, adherence to Marxism-Leninism and Mao Zedong Thought."

In practice, however, the boundaries of what can and cannot be conveyed through the mass media are constantly defended by means of censorship, altered in accord with changes in political and socioeconomic conditions, and challenged through a dynamic process of "struggle over cultural meanings and social identities."[6] The stakes of such struggles are nothing less than "the power to construct authoritative definitions of social situations and legitimate interpretations of social needs."[7] It is in the light of such struggles that we must understand the mass media as a kind of public sphere.

That mass culture plays a vital role in shaping and disseminating hegemonic ideology is an axiom of both cultural studies and official CCP policy towards the mass media in China. The presence of the mass media in the lives of China's inhabitants is pervasive. The majority of both urban and rural households have access to either television or radio. Films are

---

[5] Stuart Hall, "Encoding/Decoding," in *Culture, Media, Language,* Stuart Hall, et al., eds., (London: Hutchison, 1980), 137. As cited in Ray Pratt, *Rhythm and Resistance: Explorations in the Political Uses of Popular Music,* (New York: Praeger, 1990), 9.

[6] Nancy Fraser, *Unruly Practices: Power, Discourse, and Gender in Contemporary Social Theory,* (Minneapolis: University of Minnesota, 1989), 6.

[7] Ibid., 6.

distributed nationwide through a system of urban theaters and rural projection teams. Magazines, popular literature, and audio-cassettes are common even in isolated rural markets.[8]

As CCP cultural officials have explicitly recognized throughout the forty-year history of the People's Republic of China, such a broad distribution network lends the mass media enormous utility as a tool of ideological persuasion and popular mobilization.[9] By de-emphasizing "regional and class variation," mass culture aids in the creation and maintenance of a national community.[10] By reflecting the intellectual and cultural life of a nation, mass culture helps to forge national self-conceptions and national concerns. In portraying social relations and individual behavior, mass culture participates in defining their actual forms.

These hegemonic boundaries are maintained through both overt censorship and exclusion. This responsibility has been delegated to three government agencies: the Ministries of Propaganda (*Xuanchuan bu*), Television and Broadcasting (*Guangbo dianshi bu*), and Culture (*Wenhua bu*). In addition to these state organs, restrictions on popular music performances are often levied by city governments. In terms of its everyday workings, censorship is carried out by the CCP cadres attached to each cultural production unit. Like the Propaganda Chief in Liu Suola's "A Superfluous Story," these men and women are responsible for either approving, altering, or banning the popular songs produced or distributed under the jurisdiction of their unit, be it a record company, a performance troupe, or a television station.

Overt censorship of popular music usually takes the deletion of ideologically unacceptable lyrical content as its primary goal. This focus stems partly from the notorious difficulty of analyzing the ideological content of music purely in musical terms, and partly on account of a traditional valorization of textuality. The comments of the *tongsu* songwriter Li Lifu reflect this faith in the expressive capacity and social utility of lyrics:

> One reason pop music is able to reflect the state of society is lyrics. They are the easiest form of communication for people

---

[8] Audio-cassettes outnumber vinyl records and compact discs by a ration of ten to one. See Paul David Friedlander, "Rocking the Yangtze: Impressions of Chinese Popular Music and Technology," *Popular Music and Society*, Volume 14: 1 (Spring 1990), 66.

[9] Clark, 57.

[10] Clark, 58.

to really accept and digest, so they are very important in terms of the content and the educational value of pop music.[11]

This censorial strategy, however, is far less prevalent than the simple exclusion of ideas, attitudes, or behavior that are perceived to be beyond the ideological pale. The exclusion of rock musicians from appearing on television—be it because of objectionable lyrical content or more subtle factors like performance style—is the most prominent example of this form of censorship.

Exclusionary practices also serve to underline the 'invisibility' of the workings of cultural hegemony. In mandating that certain cultural forms remain inaccessible to mass audiences, their exclusion comes to seem normative. The fact that the hegemonic is usually identical with the normative, with all that seems natural and unquestionable about the social order, creates another form of censorship: self-censorship. Songwriters who are fully aware of what kinds of expression are permissible are unlikely to stray outside of those bounds, either because they themselves accept the boundaries as natural, or for fear of being punished by the authorities under whose jurisdiction they work.

The television documentary series *River Elegy* (*He shang*) is the most striking example of the way in which the mass media have functioned as a forum in which struggles for cultural hegemony have been enacted in China's 'new era.' *River Elegy*, written by the prominent intellectuals Su Xiaokang and Wang Luxiang, presented an attack on the despotism of Chinese political culture through a 'deconstruction' of deeply cherished symbols of the Chinese nation like the Great Wall.[12] The film advocated continued economic reform and democratization as the only means of destroying China's moribund traditional culture, while rebuilding itself as a powerful, modern nation.

In June 1988, the film was broadcast by CCTV in six parts to an estimated audience of several hundred million people, sparking an unprecedented public debate that involved nearly every medium for mass communication. Newspapers and journals throughout the country published articles on the film; book publishers issued editions of the script and

---

[11] Han and Jones, interview with Li Lifu.

[12] Alice De Jong presents a detailed and revealing account of the film's production and reception in "The Demise of the Dragon: Backgrounds to the Chinese Film 'River Elegy'", *China Information*: Vol. 4, No. 3 (Winter 1989-1990), 28-43. A transcript of the program has been published as Su Xiaokang and Wang Luxiang, *Heshang*, (Hong Kong: Joint Publishing Company, 1988).

compilations of critical writings on the film. *River Elegy* videotapes began to be sold in Beijing. Universities sponsored *River Elegy* discussion groups. Finally, as I discuss in some detail later, the ideology articulated by *River Elegy* was both influenced by and left its mark on popular music. In short, the film became an exceptional example of how, and to what effect, the mass media can function as an arena for discussion of issues of national concern.

At the same time, the *River Elegy* phenomena is indicative of the fact that the public sphere remains hemmed in by the hegemony of the CCP, and is created through a complex process of struggle. The film's broadcast on CCTV was itself a contentious issue; the Deputy Director of CCTV, Chen Hanyuan, expressed surprise that he had not been fired for airing the series without having submitted it for comprehensive review by CCTV's censorship commission.[13] Following the broadcast, the film was attacked sporadically on the grounds that its calls for political reform and "total Westernization" (*quanpan xihua*) went beyond the bounds of the "Four Cardinal Principles." In August of 1988, an altered version of the film was re-broadcast. Sections of the film directly criticizing CCP policy were deleted, as were "suggestions that Leninism is erroneous or that the CCP is losing its credibility among the population."[14] Following the suppression of the student movement of 1989, the ideological boundaries of what could and could not be said in the public sphere shrank considerably; *River Elegy* came under direct and sustained attack (in part for its connection with the reformism of the discredited General Secretary of the CCP, Zhao Ziyang) and was banned.[15]

Popular Music and the Private Sphere

Popular music's participation in the public sphere, however, takes place not only on an exclusively discursive level, but also on *musical* terms. The roots of popular music lie in dance. Listening to music is a profoundly physical experience; before music affects society as a corporate body, it is enjoyed as rhythm and movement by individual bodies. The pleasure of music, as Barthes has argued, is "essentially erotic;" we respond

---

[13] De Jong, 30.
[14] Ibid.
[15] For a compendium of critical attacks on *River Elegy*, see Hua Yan, ed., *Heshang Pipan* [Criticizing *River Elegy*], (Beijing: Wenhua yishu chubanshe, 1989).

to the materiality of sound, to the "grain of the voice," before we set about interpreting the significance of a song's lyrics.[16] Cui Jian has commented:

> The real contribution made by rock music lies in physical pleasure. It lets your arms and legs enjoy, so that your brain doesn't have to control them anymore. The brain admits that all the things your arms and legs need are natural, are beautiful.[17]

This physical pleasure, in turn, gives rise to the fact that music—as opposed to written discourse—is uniquely intertwined with private life, with the realm of emotion and desire. While I lack both the space and the expertise to discuss the psychology of music in any detail, a few general comments are in order. The experience of listening to music, by virtue of its materiality, both surrounds our bodies in any given listening environment and structures our experience of time in terms of its rhythms. At the same time, sound is evanescent—each note is itself a process of attack and decay. The ambiguities of analyzing music have been insightfully treated by Barthes, who asserts that in the face of music, our attempts at rational interpretation are often reduced to the realm of the merely adjectival. We can describe music, but our words seem to hover around the thing-in-itself, around the sheer physicality of the experience.[18] In this sense, the physical space circumscribed by music remains somewhat 'empty,' providing a receptacle into which we may invest our emotional energies. From these affective investments, we derive a sense that the music has somehow voiced our own desires, and (if only symbolically) gratified them.

Everyday life in China is full of such 'empty spaces.' Popular music is enjoyed not only at home and in the theater, but in an astonishingly large variety of social contexts. Live and recorded music is played in dance halls, restaurants, cafes, and bars, and broadcast over loudspeakers on the train, in parks, tourist sites, even Buddhist temples. Urban record shops and beauty parlors routinely pour amplified popular music into sidewalks and market areas. The increasing availability of the portable cassette player is perhaps most symptomatic of the existence of private musical space within public spaces.

---

[16] Frith, 164.

[17] Cui Jian, as quoted in Ping Fang and Ma Mu, "Yiwu suoyou: Zhongguo yaogun gexing Cui Jian" [I have nothing: Chinese rock star Cui Jian], *Xiju shijie*, 1990/ 3-4, 6.

[18] Barthes, in Frith and Goodman, 293.

As a result, listening to popular music tends to be both repetitive and distracted. We hear—but do not necessarily listen closely to—a 'hit' song over and over again in the context of many different public activities and emotional states. Through repeated listening and affective investment, popular songs become a "repository of a vast range of private associations."[19] At the same time, our 'distracted' listening habits ensure that this psychological assimilation of what is often 'background noise' often goes unexamined.

Popular songs, however, are not empty of content. Nor do they exist in a socio-cultural vacuum. Instead, their content is the product of a complex process of mediation, censorship, and struggle within the culture industry itself. The way their content is 'read' by listeners, moreover, is to some extent shaped by how it is presented within the public sphere, i.e., what is written about popular music in the *People's Daily*, or how it is presented within the format of a televised song contest on CCTV.

Song lyrics are one important focus of this process, and their reception by listeners is also informed by affective investment. By utilizing both colloquial and poetic language to express common themes of love, work, and social commentary, lyrics straddle the realms of private emotion and public sentiment. Popular lyrics invite us to identify our own passions with those of the singer, while simultaneously compelling identification with the larger realm of communal language, cultural convention, and shared emotion of which the song is only a part.

In the light of these observations, several important characteristics of the way in which popular music functions as a vehicle of cultural and political ideology are thrown into relief. First, popular music is perhaps the only mass medium in which important issues of national concern are directly figured in terms of individual desires and private life. As I will argue throughout the paper, an analogous fusion of national and individual concerns lies at the heart of the ideological concerns of *tongsu* music and underground rock. In the former, struggles are waged over the "ideological trends" that have pervaded the mass culture of the 'new era'—cultural introspection, roots-seeking, and the dilemmas of modernization evoked by the *River Elegy* debate. Rock music has grappled with many of the same themes by means of a fundamentally different sensibility and within the bounds of a different sort of public sphere: an embryonic subculture.

---

[19] Pratt, 26.

Popular Music and the Mass Culture Debate

This (necessarily reductive) model gives rise to a central theoretical dilemma in the study of mass culture in general and popular music in particular. What is the nature of the interaction between the public sphere of mass communication and private life? Is mass culture oppressive, or liberating?

> Does popular music rise from the people who constitute its audience, or is it superimposed upon them from above? Does it reflect and express their tastes, aspirations, and worldview, or does it serve to indoctrinate them, however imperceptibly, to the ideology of the class and gender which control the media?[20]

The latter argument—that mass culture is a manipulative form of social control imposed upon its audience from above—is principally associated with Marxist cultural critics of the Frankfurt School (Adorno, Horkheimer, and Marcuse).[21] The Frankfurt critique is primarily concerned with the culture industry as an agent of bourgeois ideology and capitalist "mass deception." Adorno, in a series of essays on popular music written between the 1930's and 1960's, consistently argues that the decisive characteristics of popular music are standardization and commodity fetishization. From this assumption, Adorno goes on to develop his most basic critical stance: the assertion of the homology of mass cultural standardization and the psychological world of its consumers. Pop songs are produced in assembly-line like fashion, "stream-lined" and "custom-built," while the leisure provided by pop music is simply an "after-image" of standardized work on the assembly line. In fulfilling desires already artificially manufactured by the culture industry itself, people are inescapably molded as the products of the standardized products they consume and come to "insist on the very ideology that enslaves them."[22]

---

[20] Manuel, 8. For a recent review of the mass culture debate, see Katrina Irving, "Rock Music and the State: Dissonance or Counterpoint?", *Cultural Critique* 10 (Fall 1988), 151-170.

[21] The Frankfurt School critique of popular music has not only been widely influential among scholars of popular culture, but has to a remarkable extent colored popular attitudes towards popular music. On mass culture in general, see Max Horkheimer and Theodor Adorno, "The Culture Industry: Enlightenment as Mass Deception," in *Dialectic of Enlightenment*, (New York: Continuum, 1988). For a specific discussion of popular music, see Theodor W. Adorno, "On Popular Music," in Simon Frith and Andrew Goodwin, eds., *On Record: Rock, Pop, and the Written Word*, (New York: Pantheon Books, 1990), 301-14.

[22] Ibid., 134.

In recent years, a group of predominantly British scholars of mass media and culture centered around the University of Birmingham have increasingly put Adorno's bleak assessment into question. These scholars have particularly challenged Adorno's assumption of the psychological passivity of the consumer of mass culture. Instead, they posit a process of 'recontextualization' through which listeners (particularly those involved in youth subcultures) are able to use mass cultural products for their own affective (and sometimes, political) empowerment. Scholars like Stuart Hall and Dick Hebdige have pointed out the way in which British youth subcultures have appropriated the music and imagery proffered by the mass media in order to mount challenges to hegemonic domination.[23] Whether these efforts at recontextualization are inevitably co-opted and swallowed up by the culture industry, however, remains a matter of debate.

A significant example of this process of recontextualization can be seen in the phenomena of "jail songs" (*qiu ge*) in China. These songs, based on the experience of convicts in labor reform camps, juvenile delinquents, and the rusticated youth of the Cultural Revolution, enjoyed wide popularity throughout the winter of 1988 and spring of 1989, accounting for an estimated 300,000 units of cassette sales (a relatively large figure for China's fledgling cassette industry).[24] This craze for "jail songs" was created by accident. A state-owned audio-visual publisher released a "jail song" collection which, entirely unexpectedly, sold out immediately.[25] Other production units, motivated by the need to "serve the people's currency," quickly offered their own, frequently shoddy, collections of "jail songs." The widespread rumor that such songs were disapproved of by the authorities helped to spur on even greater sales. Indeed, as a critical article appearing in *People's Music* attested, the CCP did disapprove of the cynicism and despair evoked by the lugubrious tales of crime and social ostracism contained within many of the most popular "jail songs."[26] That state-owned units persisted in producing and distributing the music is testimony to the liberalization of cultural policy occasioned by the

---

[23] See Stuart Hall and Tony Jefferson, eds., *Resistance Through Rituals: Youth Subcultures in Post-war Britain*, (London: Hutchison, 1976).

[24] Ling Xuan, "Xibei feng yu qiu ge" ["The 'Northwest Wind' and 'Jail Songs'"], *Renmin yinyue*, 1989/ 5, 38.

[25] A representative example of the "jail songs" style is Hei Taiyang [Black Sun], *Qiu ge: 68-69 zhiqing*, [*Jail songs: educated youth of 68-69*,], Liaoning beiguo yinxiang chubanshe DF-1241, 1989.

[26] Ling Xuan, 38. For a discussion of the social disillusionment reflected by "jail songs," see the December 19, 1988 edition of *Guangming ribao*.

burgeoning importance of market forces over the ideological prerogatives of the CCP.

As Jin Zhaojun asserts, the most avid consumers of "jail songs" were China's urban private entrepreneurs (*getihu*)—who are themselves a significant product of economic reform.[27] *Getihu* are a marginalized group in contemporary Chinese society; many are indeed ex-convicts, juvenile delinquents, and rusticated youths, who upon re-entrance to mainstream society were not absorbed into the public sector. They are often exploited by the officials responsible for overseeing their activities, and looked down upon by workers employed by the public sector. For these reasons, the *getihu* have coalesced as a subcultural group, characterized by a distinct entrepreneurial ethos, and characteristic styles of behavior, dress, and music consumption that diverge considerably from the mainstream.

"Jail Songs," although clearly a mass cultural commodity produced by the state-owned network of popular music publishers, were unofficially adopted as emblematic of the marginalization and disillusionment of the *getihu*. Interestingly, this appropriation of a musical style by the *getihu* went beyond simple consumption. Privately-owned beauty parlors and restaurants effectively promoted "jail songs" by pouring them out into the streets on their stereo systems. Several 'underground' cassette production facilities, owned and operated by *getihu*, began to produce bootleg "jail songs" collections.[28] In short, a style of popular music on the open market served not to reproduce hegemonic attitudes (for instance, the scorn for private merchants created by a combination of traditional prejudice and collectivist ideology), but served as a point of self-definition and empowerment for a marginalized social group.[29]

Recontextualization, of course, need not take place within the context of subcultural resistance. All popular music listeners are to some extent engaged in a process of recontextualizing popular songs, in understanding them in terms of their own lives, desires, and frustrations.

---

[27] For an innovative sociological study of the *getihu*, see Thomas B. Gold, "Guerrilla Interviewing Among the *Getihu*," in *Unofficial China: Popular Culture and Thought in the People's Republic of China*, (Boulder: Westview Press, 1990), 175-192. As of 1988, at least twenty-six million people in China were employed by the private sector.

[28] Ling, 38.

[29] Another example of recontextualization of mass mediated information, although not to be construed as a form of resistance, is revealing of the constant interaction of private life and the public sphere. I conducted the research for this study in the summer of 1990. At that time, the World Cup soccer tournament was being broadcast over TV and radio daily, and it dominated newspaper coverage. In the course of fifteen interviews, no less than half of the interviewees framed responses to questions about their lives in terms provided by the athletic events and personalities of the tournament.

This process of reception, to borrow the terms of the useful typology first proposed by Stuart Hall in relation to television viewing, and later applied to popular music reception by Ray Pratt in his study of the politics of popular music, can be either hegemonic, negotiated, or emancipatory. Hegemony is usually defined as "a ruling class's domination of subordinate classes and groups through the elaboration and penetration of ideology (ideas and assumptions) into their common sense and everyday practice; it is the systematic...engineering of mass consent to the established order."[30] Hegemonic uses of popular music, then, are those that passively accept hegemonic lyrical content without question. The second category, negotiated uses, is probably the most common, as well as the most complex and revealing in terms of struggles for cultural hegemony. They "accord the privileged position to the dominant definitions of events while reserving the right to make a more negotiated application to 'local conditions.'"[31] In Pratt's view, a negotiated use is usually a "tolerated or legitimate way of expressing accumulated feelings of anger, resentment, sexual desire." What worries many Western Marxist cultural critics is the fact that negotiated uses may function as a safety valve, as a way for oppressed groups to "let off steam" through a "substitute world of music," without confronting the social mechanics of domination *per se*.[32] The appropriation of "jail songs" by private entrepreneurs is arguably one example of a negotiated use of popular music, as are potentially many of the uses of rock music by its audiences, particularly in the context of performances.

Emancipatory uses are subversive of hegemonic codes in that they aim at an increase of the freedom and well-being of oppressed groups, often in tandem with direct political action. The Tiananmen movement of 1989 provides some especially striking examples of the emancipatory use and recontextualization of popular music. The broadcast station established in Tiananmen Square by the Beijing Autonomous Worker's Federation routinely broadcast satirical lyrics (usually openly contemptuous of the CCP's ruling elites) set to the melodies of *tongsu* songs.[33] Demonstrators adopted the lyrics of Cui Jian's seminal rock song, "I Have Nothing" as a marching chant. On at least two occasions, rock bands performed for

---

[30] Pratt, 9.
[31] Hall, "Encoding, Decoding," 137.
[32] Pratt, 12.
[33] Lu Jinghua, lecture, New England China Seminar, Harvard University, April 30, 1990.

hunger-striking students at Tiananmen Square.[34] The "March of the Volunteers" (China's national anthem) and the "Internationale"—both considered to be *tongsu yinyue* , or mass music in the tradition of Nie Er and Xian Xinghai—were used by students and workers as anthems of "democracy and freedom," and as potent symbols of the literal appropriation of patriotic and populist ideological space usually claimed as the exclusive domain of the CCP.

While Pratt's typology was originally proposed for the analysis of consumers' responses to popular music (and mass cultural products in general), such analysis is not of primary concern to this study. Instead, I would like to apply this typology to the various contextual realms I proposed in the first chapter (i.e. the circumstances of production, dissemination, performance the self-perceptions of musicians, critical discourse, as well as the lyrical content and musical styles which are produced under these circumstances) in order to understand ideology as it relates to generic differences. I begin, in this chapter, by analyzing *tongsu* music in terms of the first two categories, hegemonic, and negotiated. In doing so, I propose a different reading of the term "negotiated," stressing the actual process of negotiation and struggle in the production of popular music, and their relation to larger struggles taking place in the 'new era'. The outcome of these negotiations, because of their imbrication with the apparatus of *tongsu* music production and dissemination, are by definition never emancipatory. Instead, they produce musical and lyrical content that "accords the privileged position to the dominant definitions of events while reserving the right to make a more negotiated application to 'local conditions.' These 'local conditions' can be broadly understood in terms of the varying (and often heterodox) ideological trends referred to by Li Lifu. My primary example of negotiated uses and content in popular music will be drawn from the involvement of *tongsu* music in the controversy surrounding the television series, *River Elegy*. In chapters four and five, I will examine rock as a genre exhibiting both oppositional and negotiated elements.

Hegemonic Content in *Tongsu* Music

I now turn to an examination of the ways in which the cultural hegemony of the CCP manifests itself in the production of *tongsu* music.

---

[34] Interview with Liu Xiaosong, Beijing, June 29, 1990. For a photographic record of one of these performances, see Human Rights in China, *Children of the Dragon: The Story of Tiananmen Square*, (New York: Collier Books, 1990), 102.

As the songwriter Li Lifu asserts, the majority of popular music production in China is expressly geared to the needs of political propaganda. These needs, of course, change over time in accord with the political policies and current slogans of the CCP. Accordingly, I will examine hegemonic uses on the part of the CCP of popular music during the first half of 1990.

For cultural officials and workers in the field of ideological education, the role ascribed to popular music is reminiscent of the top-down approach to mass communication with which theorists like Adorno found themselves at odds. If the content of the music is "healthy," popular music will be conducive to the "construction of a modern socialist spiritual civilization with Chinese characteristics." If the music's content "panders to the unhealthy tastes of the masses," young listeners will be led astray from the path of socialist rectitude and morality.[35] A list of themes that must be excluded from popular music in order to prevent the distortion of popular tastes includes "sexual songs, nihilistic songs, morbid songs, violent songs," as well as any songs that transgress the ideological boundaries of the 'Four Cardinal Principles.'[36]

What sort of songs, then, are ideologically healthy? *Songs [Gequ]*, a magazine distributed nationwide by the Chinese Musicians Association (*Zhongguo yinyuejia xiehui*), devotes itself to publishing the output of China's *tongsu* songwriters, and is thus a good place to begin our examination of the nature of hegemonic content in Chinese popular songs. The songs printed in the magazine between March and June of 1990—many of which had been featured on the annual CCTV "Spring Festival Celebration" program—reveal some of the pressing ideological concerns of the CCP in the wake of the unrest of 1989. There is a marked emphasis on patriotism, stability, and normalcy. Patriotic tunes and songs in praise of the CCP predominate. Titles include "China, China, I Love You" (*Zhongguo, Zhongguo, wo ai ni*), "Our Banner is Communism" (*Women de qizhi shi gongchanzhuyi*), "The Communist Party Brings Good Times" (*Gongchandang dailai hao shiguang*), "The Motherland Gives Us Ideals"

---

[35] The participants of a scholarly conference on popular music conducted by the editors of *Yinyue yanjiu* and the Graduate School of Music of the Central Conservatory of Music were particularly concerned by the role of commercialization in lowering ideological standards in popular music. See Editors of *Yinyue yanjiu*, 23. On the role of popular music in contributing to juvenile delinquency, see Zhang Hailong and Zhang Li, "Cong 'Meimei ni da dan de wang qian zou' xiangdao de: tan yinyue jianshang yu sixiang zhengzhi gongzuo" ["Thinking from 'Sister, Go Bravely Forward': On music appreciation and ideological education work"], *Yinyue shenghuo*, 1989/7, 3-4.

[36] Ma Dongfeng, "Lai ye congcong, qu ye congcong: tongsu getan xiankuang pouxi yu sikao" ["Easy come, easy go: analysis and ideas on the current state of the popular music scene], *Yinyue shenghuo*, 1990/3, 4.

(*Zuguo gei wo lixiang*), "Motherland, Because of You" (*Zuguo, yinwei ni*), and "My Beloved Motherland" (*Wo qin'ai de zuguo*). The clearest reference to the democracy movement itself is a song that praises the military police who contributed to imposing martial law upon Beijing beginning in June 1989. The song is titled "The Song of the People's Military Police" (*Zhongguo renmin wuzhuang jingcha zhi ge*); its lyrics liken the armed police to the sun that brings happiness and joy to the people.[37] This kind of content, of course, may or may not be accepted at the level of reception, and the absence of these songs from the cassette market (despite having been featured on television) is a significant indicator that they are commercially unviable.

Indeed, market forces have presented the greatest threat to the CCP's maintenance of ideological control over *tongsu* music production. "The Valiant Spirit of Asia," (*Yazhou xiongfeng*) a song engineered to mobilize popular support for the 11th Asian Games, represents an effective attempt to overcome this problem, to popularize propaganda. As part of a massive propaganda campaign that enlisted the efforts of every mass medium, as well as festooning literally every block of every major urban area in China with Asian Games slogans, the CCP commissioned a group of prominent songwriters and singers to produce a collection of songs in support of the effort. "The Valiant Spirit of Asia," was written by China's most successful songwriting team (the composer Xu Peidong, and the lyricist Zhang Li), and features a duet between two of its most renowned pop stars (Liu Huan and Wei Wei). Its lyrics evoke the organic unity of all Asian nations, while simultaneously proclaiming China's ability to act as a successful host to the Asian Games:

> Our Asia, the mountains are its exalted head
> Our Asia, the rivers flow like warm blood
> Our Asia, the trees are like a full head of hair
> Our Asia, even the clouds shake each other's hands
> The wilderness is tied to the green-belt,
> The fields weave a swath of patterned silk
>
> As the wind of Asia springs up for the first time
> The valiant spirit of Asia shakes the sky
>
> Our Asia, the rivers and mountains are so lovely

---

[37] *Gequ*, 1990/5, 3.

Our Asia, its products are also abundant
Our Asia, its people are the most hardworking
Our Asia, its athletes are even more admirable
We will entertain guests from the four seas
We will make friends on five continents

As the wind of Asia springs up in all directions
The valiant spirit of Asia fills the sky[38]

What exactly was the song trying to accomplish as an ideological message? Out of a heterogeneous, fractious Asia (composed of nations as culturally divergent and geographically far-flung as Pakistan, Japan, and Indonesia), the lyrics construct a unitary "body," complete with head, hands, hair, and blood. Further, the Asia presented by the song is conflated with the East Asian "economic miracle," with "hard working," newly industrialized nations like South Korea, Taiwan, Singapore, and (more recently) Thailand. China itself becomes not only an equal among these nations (which in terms of economic development, it clearly is not), but occupies a privileged position as host and unifier. "The Valiant Spirit of Asia" describes not "our Asia," but China's Asia: the valiant spirit of Asia will "fill the sky" only through the good graces of Beijing's hospitality. This point becomes particularly clear in the confusion of voice manifest in the transition between the lines, "Our Asia, its athletes are even more admirable/We will entertain guests from the four seas." Whose Asia? Who is entertaining? Ultimately, the song has less to do with pan-Asian sentiment than the assertion of a Chinese nationalism badly damaged by the floundering of its modernization campaign in the wake of Tiananmen.

This interpretation is borne out by the fact that the 11th Asian Games were quite clearly an effort on the part of the CCP to re-establish the international standing and credibility of the People's Republic in the wake of the June 4th incident. They also represented an opportunity to earn significant amounts of foreign exchange earnings for a lagging tourism industry. Finally, and perhaps most vitally, they were an opportunity to restore faith on the part of the populace in the policies and viability of the CCP. The necessity of raising morale may be illustrated by the results of a poll conducted by Beijing Normal University during the course of the democracy movement, in which 95.4 per cent of Beijing's population were either "extraordinarily supportive" (50.9%) or "sympathetic"(44.5%) to the

---

[38] Assorted artists, *Yazhou xiongfeng: di shiyi ju yayun hui gequ* [The valiant spirit of Asia: songs of the 11th Asian Games], Zhongguo guangbo yinxiang chubanshe BM-025, 1990.

student movement. While the government claimed the movement was orchestrated by a small number of counter-revolutionaries, 44.6% of citizens polled attributed the movement to "inappropriate government policies," and 71.2% cited "widespread corruption".[39] The effort to mobilize patriotic pride through the Asian Games may well be seen as a method of raising morale, while sidestepping substantive economic and political issues.

In terms of musical style, the song suggests that some correspondences may be drawn between musical style and the ideological objectives of music. While largely set in the more youth-oriented, westernized idiom of *liuxing yinyue* (i.e. replete with synthesizers, rock-inflected 4/4 time, electric guitars, and what most Chinese would characterize as a "*liuxing*" singing style), the song self-consciously harkens back to the tradition of revolutionary song established by Nie Er and Xian Xinghai. The melody is pentatonic, and accompanied by both a string section and trumpets that contrapuntally echo the vocalists.

The introductory measures of the song emphasize this use of contrasting musical codes. The first two measures begin with a simple melodic figure sung by a female voice, backed by portentous synthesized percussion effects. Suddenly, a martial orchestra lurches into a homophonic fanfare, which is immediately followed by a rock beat, and a wash of strings stating the main melodic theme. The verse structure of the song is meticulously organized along a pattern of nine, five, and seven syllables per a line, echoing almost exactly the structure of many popular patriotic, revolutionary songs of the 1950's.[40] Stylistically, then, the song is both trying to evoke the exhortatory patriotism of the revolutionary song tradition, while ensuring success in the marketplace through a thoroughly contemporary pop setting.

The question remains, however: was "The Valiant Spirit Of Asia" successful in mobilizing popular support for the Asian Games? Short of detailed empirical analysis of consumer's reactions, it is difficult to ascertain the political effects of the song. Certainly, the song was often laughed off by its listeners; contemporary news reports suggest little popular

---

[39] Poll Work Group, Psychology Department, Beijing Normal University, "Beijing Public Opinion Poll on the Student's Demonstrations," translated by Woei Lien Chong and Fons Lamboo, *China Information*, Vol. 4, No. 1 (Summer 1989), 99.

[40] To cite just two classic examples: "Meiyou xin Gongchandang jiu meiyou xin Zhongguo" [No Communist Party, then no new China], music and lyrics by Huo Xin, or "Shehui zhuyi hao"[Socialism is good], music by Huan Zhi and lyrics by Xi Yang. Recordings can be found on "Zhonghua Renmin Gongheguo guoge" [The national anthem of the People's Republic of China], Zhongguo changpian gongsi HL-314, 1984.

enthusiasm in Beijing for the financial burdens imposed on them by the Asian Games. The ubiquity of the song—it was routinely played, for instance, over public address systems on trains—perhaps rendered any sort of sustained oppositional reading of its content psychologically difficult, if not impossible. Instead, the song may have become an accepted, unquestioned fixture of the public landscape, thus participating in the setting of hegemonic boundaries.

Negotiated Content: "Roots-seeking" and *River Elegy*

Hegemonic boundaries, however, are often contested, defended, and redrawn. These processes—what I will term a kind of negotiation—is the focus of the final section of this chapter. Negotiated content in popular music is produced against the backdrop of the discursive interactivity of the public sphere. The *River Elegy* debate, for instance, involved every mass medium, as have subsequent attacks on the film. *River Elegy*, in turn, was inspired by a larger movement of "cultural reflection" and "roots-seeking," that has made its presence felt in literature, cultural criticism, television, film, and popular music. Su Xiaokang's own comments on the genesis of *River Elegy* are instructive in this regard:

> This culture fever (*wenhua re*) eventually even led to a new idea, called neo-authoritarianism (*xin quanwei zhuyi*): it was hoped that a strong man would emerge from within the Party's ranks, who would be capable of genuinely implementing the reform policies. This demonstrated that the intellectuals had not grasped the crucial point of China's problems, which was that the entire society had become utterly stagnant due to ideological constraints. It was as a result of this that everyone had become extremely nervous and alarmed. A number of songs were very popular at that time. One was a song from the film *Red Sorghum*: "Sister, Go Bravely Forward", and the other was "I Have Nothing" by the young singer Cui Jian. These songs were sung in a frenzied and unbridled way, like rock-and-roll. It was a reflection of the mood of anxiety, of deadlock, and it was against this background that we conceived the plan to make *River Elegy*. Of course, as authors we were influenced by the prevalent mood. We wanted to explain what was behind these feelings of alarm and tragedy, and in a very

natural manner, we traced them back to problems of Chinese culture.[41]

This cultural anxiety revolved around two thematic axes, both of which are central to a number of 'new era' literary texts, films, popular songs, as well as *River Elegy* itself. For many Chinese writers and film-makers the dilemmas of modernization have manifested themselves in desire to reconcile tradition and modernity through "roots-seeking." Adopting Nietzsche's dictum—"Man today, stripped of myths, stands famished among all his pasts and must dig frantically for roots"—"roots-seekers" comb through remote areas and eras in search of the continuity of Chinese culture which they believe to have been severed by the onslaught of both Western and Chinese Communist culture.[42] The first axis, then, is temporal; roots-seekers (including writers like A Cheng and Han Shaogong, as well as "fifth-generation" filmmakers like Chen Kaige and Zhang Yimou) continually shuttle between tradition and modernity.[43] With the aid of modernist borrowings from the West, these writers and filmmakers endeavor to "dissect and analyze traditional cultural psychology."[44] As the literary critic Liu Zaifu has made clear, in the course of "embracing the old" (*huai jiu*), roots-seekers have brushed up against the threat of a traditional culture intractably resistant to change:

> They may take a region untouched by [modern] civilization as the background to one of their works, then lay bare its superstable psychocultural state...in their description we seem to see a brackish pool cut off from the dynamic current of modern civilization. In this pool lurks a giant, sinister

[41] W.L. Chong, "Su Xiaokang On His Film "River Elegy", *China Information*, Vol.4, No.3 (Winter 1989-90), 46. Su also cites an 'emancipatory use' of the revolutionary song "The East is Red" as evidence for this societal anxiety. The original text of the song reads, "The East is red/the sun is rising/In China, a Mao Zedong has appeared/He plans to bring the people happiness/He is the people's Great Saviour!" A parody circulating in Hunan province went, "The West is red/ The sun is setting/ In China, there is now a small guy Deng/ He is after his own profit/ And says we should each look after ourselves." Chong, 45.

[42] Friedrich Nietzsche, trans. Walter Kaufmann, *The Birth of Tragedy*, (New York: Vintage Books, 1967), 136.

[43] Many "fifth generation" films have been adaptations of "roots-seeking" fiction. A Cheng has had two novellas put on the silver screen by "fourth" and "fifth generation" directors: *King of the Children (Haizi wang*, dir. Chen Kaige, Guangxi Film Studio, 1987) and *Chess King (Qi wang*, dir. Teng Wenji, Xi'an Film Studio, 1988). Both relate the experiences of rusticated youths during the Cultural Revolution. Other "roots-seeking" stories made into films include Zheng Yi's *Old Well [Lao jing*, dir. Wu Tianming, Xi'an Film Studios, 1987], and Mo Yan's *Red Sorghum [Hong gaoliang*, dir. Zhang Yimou, 1987].

[44] Miao Junjie, "A Preliminary Study of Literary Schools in the New Era," *Chinese Literature*, Winter 1988, 182.

shadow of the specter of history, immovable and ineradicable as the stump of an ancient wall uneroded by countless rains.[45]

This dilemma has also been mapped in geographical terms, most explicitly by the writers of *River Elegy*. China's northwestern plateau (a region including Shanxi, Shaanxi, and Gansu provinces and usually referred to as *Shanbei*) occupies a fittingly contradictory place in the imagination of "roots-seekers," for it is seen at once as an almost mythical source of Chinese civilization, and as the most backward of all China's rural areas. If the *Shanbei* region is the "birthplace of the Chinese people," then the Yellow River that flows through its center is its most distinctive symbol. As the "fifth generation" film director Chen Kaige has commented on the making of *Yellow Earth* (*Huang tudi*):

> [In northern Shaanxi, the Yellow River] is broad, deep, and unhurried. It makes its stately progress through the hinterlands of Asia, its free spirit and serene depths somehow symbolic of the Chinese people—full of strength, but flowing on so deeply, so ponderously...The Yellow River flows through here in vain, unable to succor the vast barren wastes which have made way for its passage. This sight impressed on us the desolation of several thousand years of history...[46]

The "specter of history", it seems, lurks in the brackish pool of *Shanbei* culture, as well as in the Yellow River itself.

The symbolic nature of the river has been given yet another articulation in *River Elegy*, where it comes to symbolize the tragedy of a culture that has died young. The writers of *River Elegy* argue that in order to survive, China must abandon an irretrievably flawed tradition (embodied by the loess plateaus of the Northwest) and turn its attention outward to the economically vibrant southeastern coast, and by extension, the West. The final scene of the series juxtaposes an image of the Yellow River pouring out into the China Sea, overlaid by a narrator advocating continued economic reform and democratization.[47] The course of the river—from barren, landlocked, and "primitive" Northwest to the innovative, rapidly developing eastern seaboard—is in some sense also the trajectory followed

[45] Liu Zaifu, "Chinese Literature in the Past Ten Years: Spirit and Direction," *Chinese Literature*, Autumn 1989, 176.
[46] Geremie Barmé and John Minford, eds., *Seeds of Fire: Chinese Voices of Conscience* (New York: The Noonday Press, 1989), 259.
[47] Su Xiaokang and Wang Luxiang, 109-11.

by 'new era' culture. "Roots-seeking" fiction and films like *Yellow Earth* have attempted a difficult inland journey in order to salvage a sense of cultural identity before solutions like the one urged by *River Elegy* are implemented. "Roots-seeking" has been difficult precisely because of the anxiety that *River Elegy* may be right, that the specter of a politically "authoritarian" and culturally "stagnant" history may be malignant.

This same contradictory dynamic is imbricated in the very musical form of the *tongsu* style known as the "Northwest Wind" (*Xibei feng*), which itself largely derives from the soundtracks of film adaptations of roots-seeking writers:

> [This new form of music] takes modern western rock music— typically popular music produced under highly industrialized conditions—and Chinese folk musical culture—typically a musical culture held back by confined and insular cultural conditions—to produce the "Northwest Wind": a sinicized rock music (*Zhongguo minzuhua yaogun*).[48]

The song lyrics of the "Northwest Wind" must also be examined in the light of "roots-seeking." As I suggested earlier, song lyrics both publicize private emotions and privatize public concerns. This ambiguous quality is precisely what allows the "Northwest Wind" to 'contain multitudes'; to give voice to both everyday desires and the national concerns of 'new era' culture. These lyrics are inevitably set on the loess plateaus of the Northwest, and express a "roots-seeking" ethos through a contradictory set of desires to return and to escape this landscape and all that it symbolizes. These movements are usually cast in terms of the desire of young peasant women to escape the strictures of patriarchal marriage customs. More often than not, these conflicting longings can only be reconciled through the transcendence conferred on the singer by the song itself.

The song Su Xiaokang cites as having indirectly inspired the creation of *River Elegy*, "Sister, Go Bravely Forward" (*Meimei, ni dadan de wang qian zou*) is one of the most popular songs to have emerged from the "Northwest Wind" style. It was composed by Zhao Jiping for the soundtrack of the "fifth generation" film *Red Sorghum*.[49] The director of

---

[48] Jin Zhaojun, "Feng cong nali lai: ping getan xibei feng" ["Where's the wind coming from: on popular music's 'Northwest Wind'"], *Renmin ribao*, August 23, 1988.

[49] *Red Sorghum* [*Hong gaoliang*] was produced in 1987 by the Xi'an Film Studio. It is based on a story by the "roots-seeking" author Mo Yan.

the film, Zhang Yimou, wrote the lyrics in conjunction with Yang Fengliang:

> Hey! Sister, go bravely ahead, ah!
> Go forward, don't turn back your head
>
> Hey! Sister, go bravely ahead, ah!
> Go forward, don't turn back your head
> The great road that connects with the sky
> Nine thousand, nine hundred, nine thousand, nine hundred, nine, ah!
>
> Hey! Sister, go bravely forward, ah!
> Go forward, don't turn back your head
>
> From now on, you'll be building a red bridal tower, ah!
> Tossing a red bridal ball, ah!
> Hitting me right on the head, ah!
> I'll drink a pot with you, ah!
> Red red sorghum wine, ah!
> Red red sorghum wine, hey....![50]

For "roots-seekers" and the urban dwellers who gave the song its popularity, its charm lay precisely in its bucolic lack of sophistication. In the film *Red Sorghum*, the song is sung by an earthy sedan chair porter who must carry a young woman, known only as "Ninth Daughter" (*Jiu'er*), to an arranged marriage with a leprous winery owner. After an unsuccessful robbery attempt by a bandit, the porter steals a sexually charged look through the curtains of the sedan chair. Soon after, the porter ravishes Jiu'er in the sorghum fields, and the two characters embark upon a transgressive love affair. This ambiguous, highly stylized scene treads a fine line between rape and what Yingjin Zhang calls an essentially romantic "moment of desperate triumph of the 'primitive' body...over the repressive tradition of the Chinese (patriarchal society)."[51] Following this encounter, the porter

---

[50] Because of the disarray of copyright law in the Chinese popular music industry, the song has been recorded in several versions. It is performed by Zhang Yimou himself under the title "Meimei qu" [Sister song] on *Yaogun hong gaoliang* [The rocking red sorghum], Zhejiang yinxiang chubanshe ZL-156, 1988, and by Wang Di under the title "Meimei ni dadan di wang qian zou" [Sister, go bravely forward], on *Hong gaoliang* [*Red sorghum*], Guangxi minzu shengxiang yishu gongsi AB-1001, 1988.

[51] Yingjin Zhang, "Ideology of the Body in *Red Sorghum*: National Allegory, National Roots, and Third Cinema," *East-West Film Journal*, Vol. 4, No.2 (June 1990), 40.

bellows "Sister, Bravely Go Forward" over the sorghum fields. As Zhang points out, *Red Sorghum* articulates the ideology of "roots-seeking" in terms of an "ideology of the body":

> By valorizing the "primitive" way of living and the simple nature of the Chinese people—intact as they seem to be from any form of political indoctrination, *Red Sorghum* aspires to a liberation of the human body, a liberation that will return the Chinese people from their now uniform life-style and sterile way of thinking to their nurturing, regenerating origins (roots). According to director Zhang Yimou, the fast-moving pace and the celebratory mood in *Red Sorghum* are intended to awaken and return the Chinese people to their lost vitality, thus rejuvenating (the body of) the whole nation.[52]

How, then, can "Sister, Go Bravely Forward" be explained in the light of a negotiated articulation of a "roots-seeking" ideology? On the level of production, it is clearly composed of a variety of ideological trends in the public sphere, each of which have been contested and defended by critics of varying ideological stripes. *Red Sorghum* itself spurred on a series of critical debates on the nature of Chinese cultural identity almost as heated as that produced by *River Elegy*.[53] In one sense, however, it is perhaps more valuable to read the song in the context of what Pratt terms "negotiated uses" of popular music at the level of audience reception; for this is the level at which it served to inspire the genesis of further ideological contention in the guise of *River Elegy*.

The lyrics of the song are of little help in this effort; in and of themselves they signify little more than a topical (and in their approximation of a rough, rural dialect, stylistic) reference to the film. Instead, "Sister, Go Bravely Forward" must be read in terms of the eroticism implicit in Barthes' "grain of the voice." As Su's comments on the song suggest, Chinese reactions to the song were often centered on the gruff throatiness of the song's vocal tone. "Sister, Go Bravely Forward" is a song to be shouted, and its popularity lay in the fact that listeners were gratified by shouting along with the song.[54] The melodic structure of the vocal line

---

[52] Zhang, 49.

[53] For a positive and thoughtful appraisal of the film see Shi Yi, "Dianying 'Hong gaoliang' jiqi fankui" [*Red Sorghum* and its feedback], *Dianying dianshi yishu yanjiu*, 1988/8, 47-51.

[54] In this regard, I can only cite my personal experience. The song was at the height of its popularity during my stay at Beijing University in 1988-9, and it was regularly to be heard

is structured around a series of shouts and grunts; each repetition of the chorus is begun with a "hey" that lasts nearly half a measure, and each line of verse ends with a shouted "ah!". This melody, which according to the composer is loosely derived from a mixture of folk opera forms, is set over a plodding disco rhythm, and overlaid with flourishes from a typically "northwestern" instrument, the *suona* (a single reed horn).[55] The resulting mixture cannot help but to bring the participating listener to an awareness of the materiality of the body, of the sheer pleasure of shouting a tune in rhythm. Complex issues of gender are also at work here, for this kind of shouting is, both in the film and in everyday usage, an expression of the 'primitive' virility of male sexual desire. At the same time, the discursive context of the song—i.e., its links to a public debate over the organic, subjective, and liberating nature of the primitive culture from which China ostensibly arose—adds an implicit ideological dimension to the song's pleasure.

Clearly, then, singing along with the song is a way to let off steam, to express usually repressed sexual desires in a manner uncoded by the sophisticated veneer of urban life. Such an act, no matter how pleasurable, cannot ultimately be viewed as a significant challenge to cultural hegemony, remaining at most a minor and temporary assertion of subjectivity. To the extent that the song provides listeners with a much-needed emotional release, its use may indeed be seen as a negotiated containment structure for cultural hegemony.[56]

Su Xiaokang's own reaction to the song, though, did aid in the production of work that seriously challenged the boundaries of cultural hegemony of the public sphere. As I mentioned earlier, the conclusion of *River Elegy* argues for political democracy in no uncertain terms. The film praises the 1986 student movement's demands for direct dialogue with the government as an example of how politics should be open to public view and attain a degree of "transparency" (*toumingdu*).[57] This comment was excised by the CCP for the second broadcast of *River Elegy*, and ironically

bellowed out by young, male students and workers riding on their bicycles, walking on the streets, or working outdoors.

[55] Zhao Jiping claims to have drawn inspiration from Henan and Shandong *bangzi*, as well as Shanxi *qinqiang* opera. Kathryn Lowry, "Interview with Zhao Jiping," Shanxi Drama Research Institute, August 8, 1988. Unpublished manuscript.

[56] Zhang Hailong and Zhang Li cite what might be termed a "hegemonic use" of the song in their article "Thinking From 'Sister, Go Bravely Forward': On Music Appreciation and Ideological Education Work." At a crucial moment during an international ping-pong tournament, the Chinese team's cheerleaders broke into a chorus of the song, spurring their team to an important victory over the South Korea.

[57] Su Xiaokang and Wang Luxiang, 109.

(and perhaps not accidentally) became the central demand voiced by student leaders of the 1989 student demonstrations for democracy. As Dru Gladney has argued, the influence of the cultural and political theses of *River Elegy* on the student movement cannot be underestimated.[58] In this sense, the expansion of the bounds of public discourse created by *River Elegy* indirectly led to an emancipatory use of mass culture.

That these boundaries have subsequently shrunk considerably in the wake of the crackdown on that movement is attested to by the struggle in the popular music world over the ideological legacy of *River Elegy*. Where in 1987 a critic like Fan Weiqiang was free to advocate a program for the development of popular music that included increased use of political satire of the CCP and freedom from the "prescriptive power of traditional culture"—both of which echo the ideological emphases of *River Elegy*— 1990 witnessed calls for a wholesale return to the tradition of revolutionary song and mass music.[59]

"Going Towards the World" (*Zouxiang shijie*), a song that was broadcast on CCTV's 1990 "New Year's Celebration" pop music program (*Yuandan wanhui*), presents us with an unusual opportunity to observe the workings of such a shrinkage of hegemonic boundaries in the context of the censorship of popular music content. As originally recorded by the popular singer An Dong, the song was a clear response to the call for continued economic and political reform and westernization presented by *River Elegy*:

> The earth is so hungry and parched
> Fate is this bitter and painful
> As I demanded an answer of my mother
> I heard an ancient song
>
> The Great Wall isn't a shield
> The green mountains can't cut us off
> Let me go out from the perplexity of a dreamworld
> And with my steps sound out a bright song
>
> We're going towards the world in great strides

[58] Dru Gladney, "Tiananmen Revisited: Retrospection and Mediation," lecture given at the New England China Seminar, Harvard University, March 20, 1990.

[59] Fan Weiqiang, "Rang Zhongguo de tongsu gequ zouxiang shijie" [Let Chinese popular music go toward the world], *Yinyue wudao yanjiu*, 1987/11, 27-30. Interestingly, the title is also reminiscent of the closing image of "River Elegy." On efforts to revive the works of Nie Er and Xian Xinghai, see Chen Zhi'ang, "Liuxing yinyue pipan" [A critique of popular music], *Yinyue yanjiu*, 1989/4, 14-20.

Molding the great dragon's energetic vision
We're going towards the world with great strides
Rising to meet the mighty waves of the ocean

Heaven and Earth are so broad
The ocean is an expanse of gold
Just for this majestic exploration
I place my trust in the sun
The Earth will never again be tilted
The East will never again remain silent
This enduring, fragrant land sings out a surging song

We're going towards the world in great strides
Molding the great dragon's energetic vision
We're going towards the world in great strides
Rising to meet the mighty waves of the ocean[60]

The lyrics, of course, make direct reference to several of the recurring images of both *River Elegy*, and the "Northwest Wind." Just as in the final episode of *River Elegy*, a hungry, parched land must move outward towards the "ocean" and the exploratory, "sea-faring" western cultural world in order to be renewed. Further, as with *River Elegy*, these images are presented with reference to the revitalization of the cultural symbols endemic to a dead civilization. The Great Wall is no longer "a shield" holding back China's development; the "green mountains" cannot prevent China's incorporation into the modern world. As with "The Valiant Spirit of Asia," the song incorporates two different musical codes to great rhetorical effect. The initial verses are sung to the accompaniment of a minor, pentatonic melody at a very slow tempo. As if to stress the break with tradition implied by the lyrics of the chorus ("We're going towards the world in great strides..."), a double-time rock beat and a major melodic line played on a distorted electric guitar signals a distinct, and galvanizing, musical break with the verse. This structure is repeated throughout the song.

The 1990 CCTV "New Year's Celebration" roughly coincided with the release of a collection of essays devoted to comprehensively repudiating the ideological proposals of *River Elegy*.[61] Earlier, the authors of *River*

---

[60] The music was composed by Ren Zhiping, the lyrics by Wu Jiaqi. The recording is from An Dong's personal collection, as is the transcription of the lyrics.

[61] Hua Yan, ed., *Heshang pipan* [Criticizing *River Elegy*], (Beijing: Wenhua yishu chubanshe, 1989). The book was released in December 1989.

Elegy had been forced into exile for their alleged role in the 1989 democracy movement. Given these circumstances, how could CCTV countenance airing a song so inimical to current government policy? An Dong states that it was just this ideological problem which led censors at CCTV to make changes in the lyrics of the song.[62] Moreover, these changes were made with an acute awareness of the relative importance of CCTV as a disseminator of ideology—the song had previously been aired on a local station unchanged.

The alterations that were actually made provide clues to the specific concerns of CCTV officials. At the same time, they suggest that the censorship process may at times function rather inefficiently. Deleted phrases are italicized; their replacements are in boldface:

> The earth is so hungry and parched
> *Fate is this bitter and painful*
> **The mountains and rivers are this silent**
> As I demanded an answer of my mother
> I heard an ancient song
>
> The Great Wall isn't a shield
> The green mountains can't cut us off
> Let me go out from the perplexity of a dreamworld
> And with my steps sound out a bright song
>
> We're going towards the world in great strides
> Molding the great *dragon's* **giant's** energetic vision
> We're going towards the world with great strides
> Rising to meet the mighty waves of the ocean
>
> Heaven and Earth are so broad
> The ocean is an expanse of gold
> Just for this majestic exploration
> I place my trust in the sun
> The Earth will never again be tilted
> The East will never again remain silent
> This enduring, fragrant land sings out a surging song
>
> We're going towards the world in great strides

---

[62] Interview with An Dong, Beijing, June 25, 1990.

Molding the great *dragon's* **giant's** energetic vision
We're going towards the world in great strides
Rising to meet the mighty waves of the ocean

Surprisingly, there are few changes, and the central images of the song are preserved. An Dong comments that the substitution of "the mountains and rivers are this silent" for "fate is this bitter and painful" was perhaps simply a result of the former sounding "harsh." The substitution of "great dragon" (*julong*) with "great giant" (*juren*) is similarly ambiguous. It could refer to Su Xiaokang's use of the phrase "great dragon" as signifying what China's economy could be if it went "towards the world;" but from the point of view of the CCP this is hardly the most objectionable point of his argument given their continuing commitment to economic (if not political) reform.[63] The term "*juren*" may also be used to refer to great public figures, so the substitution perhaps results from the need to designate Deng Xiaoping, as opposed to an abstract symbol of the Chinese nation, as the architect of China's policies of "opening to the outside world" and economic reform.

Simply put, the censor's changes seem either arbitrary, or subtle to the point of being ineffective. Indeed, overt censorship plays a very limited role in the maintenance of hegemony in Chinese popular music. This point is perhaps borne out by the latest 'episode' in the particular ideological struggle—sparked by the broadcasting of *River Elegy* and conducted through the mass media—I have traced in this chapter:

> The latest revolutionary model television series, *On the Road: A Century of Marxism*, the Party's answer to the popular, controversial and now-banned *River Elegy* features a title song sung by the rock star Liu Huan. The lyrics are matched with images representing a short history of Chinese communism: Marx ("You're a seed of fire..."), Lenin ("a prophecy"), Mao ("a banner"), and Deng ("you spoke the truth").[64]

This, of course, is a textbook example of what might be called hegemonic recontextualization, or more simply, co-optation; i.e., the process through which potentially oppositional forms are put to the service of hegemony, and thus tamed.

---

[63] Su Xiaokang and Wang Luxiang, 105.
[64] Jaivin, "It's Only Rock 'n' Roll but China Likes It." Liu Huan also sang Xu Peidong's "The Valiant Spirit of Asia." Strictly speaking, he is not a "rock star" at all, but an amateur *tongsu* singer.

The following chapter will address the institutional restraints placed on the articulation of ideology in the production and dissemination of popular music through an examination of the lives and perceptions of many of the prominent composers, songwriters, and singers working in the *tongsu* genre.

3

TONGSU MUSIC AS A GENRE

If you sing the songs you love, the audience won't love you, and the government won't approve. If you sing the songs the audience loves, then you feel really uncomfortable. If you sing the songs the government loves, it's also...difficult...there's just no way out.

—Jing Gangshan, *tongsu* singer

This is a song of praise for a policeman shot in the line of duty. I hate singing songs like this. But I have to.

—An Dong, *tongsu* singer

These are all *our own* songs!

—Zhu Xiaomin, rock singer, beginning a performance at Beijing's Ritan Park

In the preceding chapter, I posited a model for understanding the ways in which *tongsu* music works as a vehicle for ideological struggle in contemporary China. I will now turn to the exploration of a second, closely related question: how does *tongsu* music work as *a genre*? I will consider the accounts of the genre provided by ten of the leading singers and songwriters in China in a set of interviews conducted during the summer of 1990 in terms of three of the contextual realms I proposed earlier in the book. First, the realm of production: how is the music produced? Who participates in its creation? Who controls what is sung? Second, the realm of dissemination: how does the music reach its audiences? What kind of ideological constraints does dissemination by television, cassette, or concert impose? Third, the realm of criticism and extra-musical discourse: how is the music talked about? How do these singers and songwriters see their role within these structures of production and dissemination? What kind of impact does critical discourse in the media have on their sensibilities and perceptions?

Making *Tongsu* Music

The production of *tongsu* music in China—from the composition of songs to their recording—is a complex process involving a number of highly specialized workers. Composers and songwriters collaborate in writing songs. Editors attached to audio-visual publishing companies (*yinxiang chubanshe*) select, edit (and censor, if necessary) this material for inclusion on audio-cassette releases. Finally, professional singers, musicians affiliated with state-run song and dance troupes (*gewutuan*), supervisors, arrangers, and recording engineers all participate in recording the songs for release.

This production process, although superficially similar to those of the United States or Western Europe, diverges from these more familiar models in several fundamental respects. Most obviously, production is entirely nationalized. Publishers, song and dance troupes, and recording facilities are state-owned, and state-operated. Each of these production units (*shengchan danwei*) is closely supervised by CCP officials responsible not only for the ideological content of what is produced, but the political consciousness and conduct of its employees. However, in the absence of routine state subsidization, ideological concerns must be balanced with considerations of economic profitability.

The most distinctive feature of the *tongsu* production process—one that I will argue is not only constitutive of what is distinctive about the Chinese case, but, more important, of what separates the ideology of *tongsu* music from its rock music counterpart—are its characteristic divisions of labor and power. Popular songs are written by a small group of professional songwriters, to be sung by professional singers. This institutional structure holds profound ramifications for the nature of popular music content, as well as the sensibilities of pop songwriters and singers. As Zhu Xiaomin's pointed statement at a rock performance that he *writes his own songs* indicates, this issue has also become a rallying point for the assertion of a "rock sensibility" (*yaogun yishi*) that places itself in opposition to *tongsu* music.

Songwriters

The songwriters (including both those who focus on musical composition and those who primarily write song lyrics) I interviewed in the summer of 1990 were at the pinnacle of their profession. Particularly since the huge popularity of the "Northwest Wind" in popular music, a small group of songwriters (composed of no more than 20 people) based in and around Beijing, have risen to prominence. The extent of the power they exercise over popular music production and content has led to the creation of a telling informal term for their circle, the "Northern Monopoly" (*beifang longduan*).[1]

These songwriters are usually males from thirty to forty years of age; they are members of the "lost generation" of Chinese who grew up during the decade of the Cultural Revolution. Their family backgrounds are often musical; many of their parents were also composers and songwriters. Many of them lived in remote rural areas during the late 1960's and early 1970's as part of Mao Zedong's program to rusticate and re-educate urban youth. Upon return to Beijing in the mid- and late 1970's, they received formal musical training at institutions like the Central Conservatory of Music (*Zhongyang yinyue xueyuan*). Significantly, each of them cited the revelatory impact of hearing Deng Lijun's music in 1978 and 1979 as the most important factor that swayed them towards a career in popular music— a form that had been hitherto unknown to them. Each became pioneering apprentices of popular music imported from Taiwan and Hong Kong; with continued exposure and imitation, as well as the growing availability of electrified instruments, synthesizers, and multi-track recording facilities, they were able to begin producing their own popular music by the early 1980's.[2] Their efforts were often met with government disapprobation and resistance; even for the songwriters themselves, popular music was indelibly

---

[1] Han and Jones, interview with Wen Zhongjia, Beijing, July 1, 1990. This group includes the song-writing teams of Xu Peidong and Zhang Li (responsible for a string of vastly popular tunes including "Shiwu de yueliang shi liu yuan" [The moon on the ides isn't full till the sixteenth"], "Wo relian de guxiang" [My beloved hometown], "Shi ni gei wo ai" [It's you that gives me love], "Yazhou xiongfeng" [The valiant spirit of Asia], and "Liba qiang de yingzi" [Shadows of the twig fence], and Chen Zhe and Su Yue, writers of the patriotic anthem "Xieran de fengcai" [The blood red spirit], and the "Northwest Wind" hit "Huangtu gaopo" [Hills of yellow earth]. Other important figures in the "monopoly" include the lyricist Jia Ding, and the composers Li Lifu and Wen Zhongjia.

[2] The importance of such technologies to the development of popular music cannot be overestimated. As Wen Zhongjia mentions, one of the first electric keyboards to reach Beijing was a gift from the Japanese embassy to the Ministry of Foreign Affairs in 1978. Musicians and composers literally queued up to have a chance to see and experiment with this instrument.

associated with the specters of "yellow music," imperialism, and bourgeois ideology.

By the late 1980's, however, pop music had been grudgingly accepted as a permissible form of mass culture, largely because of its enormous economic potential. Popular music had become *institutionalized*; government officials had begun to worry not about how to stem the tide of its popularity, but how to balance its inevitable commodification with ideological control. Songwriters like Xu Peidong, Li Lifu, Wen Zhongjia, and Jia Ding all contributed to the creation of the "Northwest Wind" in 1988.[3] In fusing Chinese folk melody with disco and rock rhythms, this popular style was almost universally lauded as the symbol of the end of the mainland's reliance on imitation of the musical models provided by Hong Kong and Taiwanese popular music.[4] The "northern monopoly" had been transformed from embattled pioneers of an ideologically suspect music, to the pillars of an institutionalized, state-run system of musical production.[5]

What role do these songwriters play within this system? While many are nominally employees of state-owned production units like CCTV, the Eastern Song And Dance Troupe (*Dongfang Gewutuan*), or the Institute of Chinese Opera (*Zhongguo Geju Xueyuan*), the scope of their activities is much broader than these institutional affiliations might suggest. Indeed, their activities encompass nearly every facet of *tongsu* music production and dissemination. Songs are usually written on a contractual basis for television stations, film studios, and audio-visual publishers. The lyricist Jia Ding works regularly as an editor and recording supervisor for a variety of record companies, as well as one of the principal promoters of the celebrated "One Hundred Pop Stars" (*Baiming Gexing*) concert held annually in Beijing.[6] Wen Zhongjia often orchestrates the instrumental settings and arrangements for major recording sessions, in addition to composing songs

---

[3] Ironically, the first two "Northwest Wind" songs were created by composers outside of the "northern monopoly." Xie Chengqiang, a composer from the southern metropolis of Guangzhou, wrote what was perhaps the first use of a Shanbei melodic and lyric forms with disco accompaniment in the song "Xintianyou." Cui Jian's seminal rock song, "Yiwu suoyou" [I have nothing] is also frequently cited as the first song in the "Northwest Wind" style, although Cui himself denies that it is anything but a rock song. Interview with Cui Jian, Beijing, July 31, 1990.

[4] See, for example, Jin Zhaojun, "Feng cong nali lai: ping getan Xibei feng" [Where's the wind coming from: on popular music's 'Northwest Wind'].

[5] Among the widely popular "Northwest Wind" songs created by the "northern monopoly" were "Wo relian de guxiang" [My beloved hometown] by Xu Peidong, and "Xin zhong de taiyang" [The sun in my heart] by Li Lifu.

[6] Han and Jones, interview with Jia Ding, Beijing, July 5, 1990. To cite one example, Jia Ding is listed as the supervisor for the cassette *Guaxiang 89 de da xuanfeng* [The whirlwind of '89], Zhongguo qingnian yinxiang chubanshe QN-063, 1989.

and film soundtracks.[7] Most songwriters regularly participate in the television industry, either as the writers of theme songs for television series, or in producing (or acting as judges in) televised popular singing contests.

This diversity of roles underscores the importance of songwriters as creators and "gatekeepers" of *tongsu* music content. Not only do they write songs, but they participate in their selection, censorship, recording, and broadcasting through the mass media. These are all activities from which singers and musicians are effectively barred. The question then arises: to what end do songwriters exercise these creative powers? What kinds of goals inform the content of their compositions? At this point, it will be useful to review Li Lifu's account of the occupational goals of *tongsu* songwriters in China:

> In China, songwriting can't be without some kind of objective. For *tongsu* songwriters, there are three kinds of goals. The first, and the most prevalent, comes from the government: using pop songs as tools of political propaganda. For example, there's an anti-bourgeois liberalization campaign, so everybody writes anti-bourgeois liberalization songs, or now there's certain political changes, so everybody does that, or at one time people are saying Chinese are bad too much [so officials say], "Why don't you write that Chinese are good!"..The second kind of objective is complete self-expression, which is mostly what the composers over at the conservatory are doing... The third kind are those who would like to encourage certain ideological trends. If you want to distinguish even more finely, then there are those who want to make lots of money, and those who want to flatter high officials [literally 'pat the horse's ass', *pai mapi*]...[8]

Clearly, *tongsu* songwriters must operate under constraints imposed by the CCP officials. Their work is thus caught between the rock of ideological orthodoxy and the hard place of profitability. Interviewees often spoke of the difficulty of reconciling these various demands with the imperatives of artistic expression and personal integrity.

---

[7] Wen Zhongjia arranged a best-selling collection of "Northwest Wind" songs for the Central Song and Dance Troupe (*Zhongyang gewutuan*) released as *Shanbei 1988* [Shanbei 1988], Zhongguo dianying chubanshe J-1034, 1988.

[8] Han and Jones, interview with Li Lifu.

The conflict of propaganda and artistic creativity was cited as the most damaging to Chinese popular music: some songwriters stated explicitly that the government had stunted the healthy development of popular music in China.[9] Another criticized the politicization of cultural policy, stemming from Mao's Yan'an Forum, that rendered the intertwinement of propaganda and popular music inevitable.[10] The discomfort they felt towards the imposition of ideological control was articulated both in terms of the value of artistic integrity and the bitter lessons of the totalitarianism of cultural policy during the Cultural Revolution:

> In order to serve as art, popular music must transcend popular notions of morality and law in current circulation. If they don't, art will just become a tool of the state. At the beginning of the Cultural Revolution, moral standards were summed up by one phrase: "It's right to rebel" (*zaofan you li*). But what kind of morality or law is that? What kind of art could come out of that?[11]

While Li Lifu was clearly proud of the Daoist philosophical content of his most famous composition, "The Sun In My Heart" (*Xin zhong de taiyang*), economic constraints also figured largely in his creative work:

> If my songs don't make money, I starve. I won't have new clothes, won't be able to get a haircut. So, I do two kinds of work. [Their content] is not at all alike! I won't sign my name to songs I write just to make money, but that's what I do if I run out of bread and butter, don't have any beer, or any Marlboros...[12]

---

[9] Han and Jones, interviews with Wen Zhongjia, and Jia Ding.

[10] Han and Jones, interview with San Bao, Beijing, July 15, 1990. San Bao, in his late twenties and still a student at the Central Conservatory of Music, is the youngest songwriter we interviewed. Only Li Lifu denied that government intervention had a significant impact on his work and the nature of his song's content. Interestingly, he did not deny that such intervention was widespread, but simply dismissed government criticisms of popular music as being largely ineffective. Han and Jones, interview with Li Lifu.

[11] Ibid.

[12] Ibid. These comments notwithstanding, the average income of a successful songwriter in the *tongsu* music industry is many times above that of either a construction worker, a teacher, or a doctor.

These economic and political constraints typically produce either straightforwardly hegemonic content, or material that evidences a 'negotiated' attempt to incorporate economic, ideological, and personal concerns. The work of the composer Xu Peidong and the lyricist Zhang Li, already discussed in the context of "The Valiant Spirit of Asia," is one such example. Their earlier, and almost unprecedentedly popular "Northwest Wind" song, "My Beloved Hometown" (*Wo relian de guxiang*, 1988) is a good example of 'negotiated content.' The song describes a stagnant and impoverished rural village, and its inhabitants' heartfelt desire to modernize. The song's theme *should* fit neatly into a common lyrical sub-genre, the song of praise for one's native place (*xianglian ge*).[13] As Jin Zhaojun explains, though, this conventional lyric type was instantly undercut by the song's first line in an ironic manner instantly recognizable to most listeners: "My hometown isn't pretty at all..." In its self-consciously ambiguous treatment of the intractability of rural 'backwardness,' the song arguably belongs to Li Lifu's third category—the encouragement of (not necessarily orthodox) ideological trends like "roots-seeking."

A similar complexity is evinced by the work of the songwriting team of Chen Zhe and Su Yue. Their "The Blood-stained Spirit" (*Xieran de fengcai*, 1986), because it was commonly (and according to Chen, mistakenly) thought of as a patriotic ballad praising the sacrifices of PLA soldiers who fought in border clashes against the Vietnamese throughout the late 1970's and early 1980's, was adopted by the PLA as a semi-official anthem in 1986.[14] In an interesting case of recontextualization, the song later came to symbolize the patriotic sacrifices of demonstrators in the 1989 Tiananmen movement for many residents of Hong Kong. A later song, "Hills of Yellow Earth" (*Huangtu gaopo*, 1988) elicited fierce criticism in the official music journals for its adoption of a "roots-seeking sensibility" that ignored the accomplishments of the CCP in rural modernization, and

[13] A contemporary example of a *xianglian* song is Xie Chengqiang and Zhang Quanfu's "Wo jia shi ge hao difang" [My home is a good place] on *Fantian fudi: Zhongguo xin yinyue xilie zhi er* [The world is overthrown: Chinese new waves volume two], Yongsheng yinyue chubanshe SMC 90002, 1990.

[14] Wang Hong, *Xieran de fengcai* [The bloodstained spirit], Yuesheng changpian gongsi mRCS-8026, 1990. Chen Zhe, who is now living in Hong Kong, states that the song was intended as a democratic anthem from the very start. Interestingly, he has recently started a production company in Hong Kong that aims to promote rock music from mainland China, and has released a compilation featurning Beijing rock musicians entitled *Hei yueliang ling yishuang yan kan Zhongguo* [Black Moon: The other side of China], CZ Music Production 9101, 1991. For an account of Chen Zhe's career, see Mao Sen, "Fanpan wenhua, dalu de yaogun yi zu: fang 'Xieran de fengcai' zuoci ren Chen Zhe" [[Rebellious culture, mainland rock: an interview with the lyricist of 'The blood stained spirit,' Chen Zhe], *Jiushi niandai*, 1991/9: 72-75.

perpetuated "feudal backwardness."[15] Chen Zhe himself claims he wrote "Hills of Yellow Earth" in order to make people "reflect on Chinese culture" in terms drawn from the larger intellectual movement towards "cultural self-reflection" (*wenhua fansi*) and "roots-seeking."[16] At the same time, he aimed for an artistic summation of his experiences and feelings during a trip to the rural Northwest with a CCTV film crew. In short, these songwriters' work (like that of their 1930's predecessor, Liu Lei'an) tends to accommodate within itself contradictory ideological content as a result of the complex set of personal objectives and institutional restraints through which it is created.

The inclusion of overtly oppositional content was ruled out by most of the interviewees, with one significant exception. Their jobs very clearly ride on a measure of self-censorship. Just as surely as a string of unsuccessful songs could lead to economic insecurity, a foray outside of the bounds of acceptable ideological boundaries would lead to extreme political insecurity. Only one songwriter indicated to me—off the record—that he had written songs praising student demonstrators during the Tiananmen uprising in the spring of 1989. The fate of these songs mirrors the ambiguities of ideological control in *tongsu* music. He submitted them to the editors of a state-owned audio-visual publishing house with trepidation. The songs' oppositional content was so oblique, however, that they passed unnoticed through the censorship board of the company, and were released in early 1990. The songwriter, however, felt sure that a "select audience" would understand the songs' message, despite the trappings of state approval conferred upon them by inclusion on the cassette.

Finally, songwriters readily accept the notion that their work must serve political and social ends; that it must function as a form of both ideological and moral education for the masses. Li Lifu, while disavowing the efficacy of government criticisms of popular music (and challenging the nationalist ideologies expressed by a song like "The Valiant Spirit of Asia"), firmly believed that songwriters should "guide their audiences" towards a better understanding of society, morality, philosophy, and music itself. His recognition of the pedagogic power of popular music—and the efforts of many of his colleagues to use the *tongsu* genre as a forum for

---

[15] See *Huangtu gaopo* [Hills of yellow earth], Tianjin yinxiang youxian gongsi, 1988. For critical attacks on the song, see Duan Ruanzhong, "Jigong huangtu gaopo" [An attack on 'Hills of Yellow Earth'], *Renmin yinyue*, 1989/3, 30-31.

[16] Ning Jing, "Yi wei youyu de gezhe: Chen Zhe de gushi" ["A melancholy songwriter: Chen Zhe's story"], in Wang Canqi and Han Xiaohui, eds., *Dangdai gewang* [Contemporary kings of song], (Beijing: Huafu chubanshe, 1989), 91.

'cultural self-reflection'—reflects the continuing hegemony of a firmly entrenched discursive paradigm that stretches back to the progressive songwriters of the 1930's: the socio-political instrumentality of popular music.

Singers

Such considerations of ideological instrumentality are a luxury denied to those who actually sing the songs the songwriters compose. These singers, however, are the very stuff of *tongsu* music. They, not songwriters, editors, officials, studio musicians or recording engineers, are the public figures through which *tongsu* music participates in the public sphere. As such, their voices both provide musical pleasure, and become the objects of the audience's affective investments into the music. Audience reception and consumption of *tongsu* music are structured around singers. Unlike the Anglo-American case, there are neither famous bands (like the Beatles), nor well-known singer-songwriters (such as Bruce Springsteen). Cassettes are either devoted to the work of one singer, or feature several singers grouped together by style (i.e., the "Northwest Wind") or theme ("The Stars Celebrate Spring Festival," for instance). Studio musicians remain anonymous, identified only by the particular *gewutuan* that provided the band for the recording session.

The centrality of the role of singers is reflected by the discursive practices surrounding the reception and appreciation of *tongsu* music. Everyday discussion, newspaper articles, television and radio programs on *tongsu* music are all characterized by a marked emphasis on qualities of vocal production. As I have already noted, styles within the *tongsu* genre are usually grouped together by singing style (*changfa*), not instrumental accompaniment. Singers, in turn, are categorized as representing a certain style in terms of the quality of their voices, be they "gentle" (and thus in the "lyrical" style), or "rough" (and thus belonging to the "energy song," or "Northwest Wind" style). Televised singing contests, moreover, simply feature a procession of individual vocalists, backed by a single instrumental ensemble, who are judged on the technical and emotional proficiency of their singing.

This focus on exquisite gradations of individual voices is belied by the fact that the singers themselves are hemmed in by a series of institutional constraints that ensure that their songs are literally not their own. Although songwriters, editors, and officials attached to the work units with which singers must work are the creators and controllers of the music, they remain hidden from the gaze of the public.

I now turn to a discussion of the implications of this system of *tongsu* music production by means of the material garnered from five interviews conducted with *tongsu* singers in the summer of 1990. Each of these singers is immensely popular throughout the mainland, and known to audiences that number in the hundreds of millions, largely by way of successful appearances on televised singing contests.[17] Each of them commands incomes many times above the national average. Two are males (Jing Gangshan, Liu Huan), and three female (An Dong, Hu Yue, Zhao Li); all are in their twenties. Three of the five came from families where one or both parents were musicians. Three of the five had themselves undergone some kind of formal musical training.[18] Despite their musical backgrounds, all of them characterized their success as being as a matter of a combination of "coincidence," and "good connections" (*guanxi*).

While the *tongsu* music industry is largely geared towards presenting singers to audiences, the experiences related to me by these singers reflected a sense of powerlessness and exploitation. Much of this resentment was directed towards the song and dance troupes (*gewutuan*) that are usually the primary employer of *tongsu* singers. Of the five singers, two were employed by a *gewutuan*. An Dong, like many other *tongsu* singers, is affiliated with a unit that acts as both a propaganda organ and a money-making venture for the PLA Air Force—the Song and Dance Troupe of the Air Force Political Department (*Kongzheng gewutuan*). Zhao Li is a member of a troupe loosely affiliated with CCTV, the China Broadcast Arts Song and Dance Troupe (*Zhongguo guangbo yishu gewutuan*). Both Hu Yue and Jing Gangshan elected early on in their careers to "go into the cave" (*zou xue*), abandoning the lifetime job security of affiliation with a troupe in order to work on a free-lance basis for various state-owned organizations. Liu Huan is an anomaly among *tongsu* singers. He holds an academic position teaching Western music history, and free-lances as a singer on the side.

---

[17] For brief profiles of each of these singers, see Yang Wenyong, ed., *Zhongguo gexing gequ lu* [Chinese pop stars and pop songs], (Beijing: Dongfang chubanshe, 1990).
[18] Jing Gangshan attended the high school attached to the Central Conservatory of Music. An Dong graduated from the Shanghai Conservatory of Music in 1984. Liu Huan is an assistant professor of Western music history at the Institute of International Relations.

Working in the context of a *gewutuan* is taxing, and compensations (either financial or otherwise) are few. As An Dong describes:

> Concerts and recordings are sometimes organized by the troupe. If so, you are required to sing. They pay very little, just five yuan [about $1.25 U.S.] a night. Of course, all the profits go to the unit. *The unit exploits the workers...*and they don't care about the development of your career, they don't help you make a name for yourself in the pop world... *In fact, the only thing the troupe does care about is overseeing the content of my performances and recordings.* Since most of the leaders are older, their tastes lean toward folk songs and not more westernized pop songs [*liuxing gequ*]. So if your program is all pop with no folksy touches, you will incite their disapproval and be cut down. Censorship is particularly strict in our unit because it's military.[19]

The ideological restrictions imposed by the unit extend into the daily life of the singer, and include mandatory political education meetings. More subtly, politics are sometime become a means of conducting personally motivated in-fighting within the workplace.

Because of these frustrations, most of An Dong's singing is done outside of the unit, on a free-lance basis. Like Xiao Hu in "A Superfluous Story," she is often commissioned by the 'propaganda chiefs' of television stations or audio-visual publishers to participate in recording sessions. These jobs, while financially lucrative, do not allow her any greater degree of creative freedom; instead of being subject to the demands of officials in her own unit, she is responsible to songwriters, editors, and censors of the hiring unit. Even this sort of work, though, is unavailable for less successful members of the troupe: "singers can't get famous or go on tour without their unit's permission."[20] Largely because of the greater financial possibilities offered by this kind of free-lance work, An Dong has actively attempted to retire from the Air Force unit, but as their most popular (and thus profitable) asset, her efforts have been unsuccessful.

Zhao Li's experiences within the *gewutuan* suggest that some of the problems An Dong raises are endemic to the system:

---

[19] Italics mine. Interview with An Dong, Beijing, June 25, 1990.

[20] Han and Jones, interview with Jing Gangshan.

I have no choice in what I sing. I sing what's given me, what they demand I sing. Working in the troupe, I feel controlled not so much by the censorship, but by their control over what I do with my time. To get my salary, I have to participate in a lot of activities I'd rather not.[21]

Like An Dong, Zhao Li often works free-lance. In all interviews, free-lance work seemed to be predicated on the passivity of the singer. If one is "suitable," songwriters and officials will "look you up." In no case did singers speak of actively seeking work. As with her work in the *gewutuan*, Zhao Li plays no active role in selecting songs for performance, or even the style in which she is to perform:

What I sing usually isn't expressing my real self, so it's strange that my audience is familiar only with this persona who isn't really me. They just know that I'm famous and say, "Great, great. She sings so sweetly."[22]

In short, the individual singer has very little to do with the production process; just as her voice becomes the pleasurable focus of audience attention, her own individual voice becomes something of a mouthpiece for songwriters and officials, whose presence 'behind the scenes' is elided by the mechanics of performance.

Hu Yue gives us a closer look at the procedures and problems of free-lance singing. She is proud of her independence from a *gewutuan*, and asserts that her escape from the constraints of a work unit required real courage:

I like the complete freedom. I don't have a manager. I'm my own master. But it's very difficult, very trying, especially for a woman... I've come across a lot of swindlers who said they could help me make records, but it turned out that they didn't even understand the business as well as I did... Finally, I got some exposure, and some companies liked my work well enough to keep me on as a house singer. I recorded four cassettes for Sichuan and Yunnan Audio-visual Publishers... my pay and the amount of support and guidance I got had no

---

[21] Han and Jones, interview with Zhao Li and Wo Peng, Beijing, July 3, 1990.
[22] Ibid.

correlation with how many cassettes I sold. You just get a standard fee for each, no matter how well they do.[23]

Because of the disarray of copyright law in contemporary China, singers do not receive royalties. Although singer's incomes are well above the national average, these circumstances, of course, smack of the economic exploitation An Dong identifies within the *gewutuan* system. The economic benefits of "going into the cave," Hu Yue makes clear, are dependent on the maintenance of good relations with officials, songwriters, and editors, many of whom "do their best to control the lives of performers":

> In *tongsu* music circles, particularly as a woman, you can't afford to offend anyone. You have to pay attention to these people and please them, or else you'll be in trouble.[24]

These statements call to mind the sexual harassment levied upon Xiao Hu by the Propaganda Chief in "A Superfluous Story." Indeed, Hu Yue's comments elsewhere suggested that such practices do exist in *tongsu* music circles. In "A Superfluous Story," Liu Suola points out that these exploitative conditions often create a kind of infantilization on the part of singers, which is figured in (gendered) terms of sexual violation. Blackie, a musician in Xiao Hu's band, complains about his relationship with a record producer:

> "A goddamned old lady leans on you, all the time taking advantage of the fact that she has money in her purse, that she can fucking make a tape for you, capitalizing on being the manager of such and such company! And after it's all done, she still wants me to act like her little boy." He buried his head in the sofa again,...." You're still hoping to sing with all your heart. Well, take this opportunity now and just forget about it."[25]

Jing Gangshan's profound sense of disillusion with his own work as a *tongsu* singer expressed itself in verbal gestures not unlike Blackie's burying of his head in his sofa in frustration. He almost obsessively returned to discussions of the futility of his work. Unequivocal statements of the utter lack of creative freedom allowed him by the system gave way to tentative

---

[23] Han and Jones, interview with Hu Yue, Beijing, July 6, 1990.
[24] Ibid.
[25] Liu Suola, 111.

expressions of hope, each of which were quickly squelched by a "there's no way out" (*meiyou banfa*):

> ...performances and recording sessions are arranged completely by other people. I sing in order to survive. I have no other goal, no other motivation... even if I wanted to sing a certain song, no one would let me... there's no way out.[26]

Against this bleak backdrop, Liu Huan's optimism was something of an anomaly. This is largely a result of his status as an amateur *tongsu* singer whose institutional affiliations are removed from the hurly-burly of *tongsu* music circles. Liu Huan was educated in the foreign languages department of the Institute of International Relations; he presently teaches the history of Western music at the same college. Victory in a French language singing contest, followed by his success with Li Lifu's composition "The Sun in My Heart," won him nationwide fame. Unlike most pop stars, who "want to be pop stars just to be a pop star," he professes that his motivation for singing is simply "love for the music."[27] He has begun to write his own songs, in an effort to introduce audiences to higher "aesthetic standards," to a "gentle pop sound, a bourgeois sound."[28] Despite these ideals, he too is afflicted by a measure of cynicism. He has found it impossible to have his own songs produced, citing a lack of capital. Instead, his fame has been consistently capitalized upon the authorities through his participation in the recording of songs like "The Valiant Spirit of Asia" and the title song for CCTV's response to *River Elegy, On the Road: A Century of Marxism*. Even so, he believes, echoing the imagery of sexual violation other *tongsu* singers commonly use in reference to their participation in the industry, that:

> You can't expect popular music to inspire people to fight for the four modernizations, to inspire people to emulate Lei Feng, or what have you. Popular music is an art that's been raped. Raped by ourselves.[29]

---

[26] Han and Jones, interview with Jing Gangshan.

[27] Han and Jones, interview with Liu Huan and Li Lifu, Beijing, July 21, 1990.

[28] Ibid.

[29] Ibid. Lei Feng, a model PLA soldier and selfless revolutionary, was the subject of a massive propaganda campaign that took place in the late 1960's and 70's. His image was exhumed following the crackdown on the Tiananmen movement in an effort to improve morale, and stimulate "socialist" consciousness among young people.

Performing *Tongsu* Music

There are many media for the dissemination of *tongsu* music, including television, audio-cassettes, concerts, radio, and film. Television, of course, is far and away the most important of these mass media in terms of both the sheer volume of its audience, and its consequent efficacy as an instrument of promotion and propaganda. While a successful cassette may sell as few as fifty thousand copies, the most popular of the televised singing contests reach estimated audiences of up to 700 million people, or 68 percent of the Chinese population.[30] The vastness of the television audience has several important consequences. First, it virtually guarantees the celebrity and economic success of the songs and singers who appear on annual CCTV programs like the "New Year's Celebration" (*Yuandan wanhui*), the "Spring Festival Celebration" (*Chunjie wanhui*), the "National Youth Singers Television Contest" (*Quanguo qingnian geshou dianshi dajiangsai*), or the "National *Tongsu* Song Contest" (*Quanguo tongsu gequ dajiangsai*). Second, the scope of the audience mandates extremely tight supervision of the content of the proceedings on the part of CCTV officials. Rock music is barred from such contests, and song lyrics are almost universally hegemonic, never straying far from patriotic and socialist themes. One songwriter informed me that following the suppression of the 1989 democracy movement, television authorities mandated that even songs treating "love and personal feelings" be excised from CCTV programming.[31] This strict control extends to styles of instrumental accompaniment and performance. The clothing styles and hairstyles of singers are selected by CCTV officials, and their gestures are rigidly formulaic and restrained.

What do audiences see when they watch such a contest? Does viewing offer possibilities for an empowering recontextualization of the program? As Mao Bian's description of the 1986 CCTV "National Youth Singers Television Contest" points out, the "fascination" of the *tongsu* singing contest lies both in the sheer pleasure of the spectacle and in its participatory nature (*canyuxing*).[32] The first point is transparent. Spectators are presented with a procession of up to one hundred singers, each of whom is backed with lavish sets. The participatory nature encompasses several different aspects. To the extent that the enjoyment of popular music

---

[30] Mao Bian, "How a TV Contest Captivated China: Music Lesson For Millions," *China Youth*, 1987/1, 28. See also James Lull, *China Turned On: Television, Resistance and Reform* (London and New York: Routledge, 1991), 23.

[31] Han and Jones, interview with San Bao.

[32] Mao Bian, 28-29.

is a process of affective investment, the viewer clearly engages in an active relation with the music that is presented. In the case of the televised contest, though, this relationship is constituted as a *critical* activity. Viewers cannot help but to align themselves with the twelve judges who preside over the program. A typical letter to CCTV from a viewer commenting on the program reads, "We are a family of seven. We all joined the judges in grading...we applauded when we gave marks close to the judges!"[33]

Just as the voices of the singers have been usurped by the apparatus within which they work, the critical judgement of the audience seems to be sutured to that of the judges. The pronouncements of the judges on the technical and emotive proficiency of the singers is re-constituted as the realm of the popular; "the whole of China [becomes] the theater with judges in their hundreds of millions."[34] The comments of Li Yinghai, the vice-director of the Central Conservatory of Music, substantiate the notion that the principal aim of the singing contest is to establish hegemonic boundaries of what and how *tongsu* music should communicate to its audiences:

> It was fine that the prize contest should have given guidance to *tongsu* music and set requirements for its contents, style, singing and performance gestures.[35]

At the same time, the routine exclusion of unacceptable genres and ideologies is successfully hidden from view, and elided. Indeed, exclusion comes to be seen as "coterminous with what is natural...about the social order."[36] In this light, it is difficult, if not impossible, to argue that the televised singing contest offers its audiences the opportunity for either negotiated or oppositional readings.

This pessimistic interpretation is (unfortunately) reinforced by *tongsu* singer's accounts of what transpires behind the spectacle of the televised singing contests. Interviewees reserved their fiercest criticism for the deleterious effect of the contests on the quality of *tongsu* music, their lives, and their work. This outpouring of resentment must be understood in the light of the fact that television is the only avenue to success in *tongsu* music. Record companies in China do not advertise their products in the

---

[33] Ibid., 28.
[34] Ibid., 28.
[35] Ibid., 30.
[36] Hall, 137.

mass media, and neither radio nor concerts generate large-scale publicity. As a result, the monopoly held by television is seen to have profound influence on the musical tastes of the popular audiences:

> There's only one means of popular music promotion in China—TV. And it colors people's tastes and judgements disproportionately. People just end up liking and being used to whatever's on TV.[37]

Again and again, interviewees stressed that popular success is entirely predicated on participation in televised singing contests. The opportunity to participate, in turn, is "less a matter of how much audiences like you, or how talented you are, than the connections you have, the patronage of officials and songwriters."[38] Success in the contests was also portrayed as a matter of connections:

> There is a lot of in-fighting, lots of factions. Without backing, without an organization to promote you, it's tough to make it successfully through the maze.[39]

Every one of the interviewees viewed the contests as unpleasant at best, and traumatic at worst. Hu Yue, who took the first prize in 1988 at the "Third National *Tongsu* Song Contest," describes the experience in terms that once again imply a sense of personal violation. Her appearance on the show caused a sensation, for as she was awarded her trophy after a tense run-off with another contestant, she burst into tears:

> I cried. My stomach was in knots. I couldn't speak. This was the first time a singer ever cried on live TV, but I couldn't control myself, I was overwhelmed with resentment. I had to sacrifice so much, put out so much...feelings that are particularly easy for a woman to be sensitive to. But I can't tell you any more about those things, because I'm still working in *tongsu* music circles...A lot of other singers saw what happened to me that time, saw my humiliation, but they still want to participate, just to get famous. It's an

---

[37] Han and Jones, interview with Zhao Li and Wo Peng. The same point was reiterated in interviews with Jing Gangshan, and Hu Yue. Significantly, *tongsu* songwriters did not criticize televised singing contests at all.

[38] Ibid.

[39] Han and Jones, interview with Hu Yue.

opportunity they can't pass up. Even if they lose, they'll still be exposed to a huge audience.[40]

Jing Gangshan's comments restate this predicament, once again likening the almost total control exercised by television officials over the singer to physical violation:

> Singing contests don't have anything to do with talent. I want to participate in them, but when I do I regret it. Maybe some official type will give someone a lot of money, and the points scored by the singers...it's no judge of talent anyway... Once I went on and they made me cut my hair before the show. I felt like I was being raped.[41]

As I discuss later, the central component of the 'rock sensibility' springs from a rejection of the suppression of individuality inherent in such a system of dissemination. Instead of serving as a mouthpiece of state propaganda, rock musicians claim to give voice to their own inner feelings in their own songs. Where *tongsu* singers feel their own bodies to be exploited by the machinations of the *tongsu* music apparatus, Cui Jian lauds the liberating physicality of rock music. In "A Superfluous Story," Xiao Hu's final self-realization—triggered by the sexual harassment of the Propaganda Chief—is cast in terms of an analogous reaction of disgust to television and all it stands for:

> Nor do I plan to go on TV, to win any prizes, or to be critiqued by the Chief in the newspapers. I still must tell the other people in the band... to crush our TV sets too, because they're going to broadcast a special interview with the Chief....let his wife wear her fur coat as she entertains reporters from the TV station, let the TV reporters be so moved by he and his wife's nonsense that they waste all their videotape, let them all have their secret affairs, let everybody watching TV all yell at their TV's after seeing that show— anyway, I'm going back to the workshop to do some work.[42]

---

[40] Ibid. For a printed (and somewhat sanitized) account of this incident, see Xu Xiaowu, "Hu Yue de meili: qingnian geshou Hu Yue: qiren qige" [The charm of Hu Yue: herself, her songs], in Wang Canqi and Han Xiaohui, eds., 130-2.

[41] Han and Jones, Interview with Jing Gangshan.

[42] Liu Suola, 115.

In contrast to the televised singing contest, both audio-cassettes and live concerts seem to offer a far less manipulative environment for the reception of popular music by its audiences. Several Western critics have pointed out that the wide availability of cassette technology, "offers the potential for diversified, democratic control of the means of musical production," through "backyard cassette industries [that] are able to respond to diverse regional, ethnic, and class tastes," usually neglected by corporate or state-owned enterprises.[43] Both the production of bootleg "jail song" collections by private entrepreneurs, and the widespread availability of homemade Cantonese pop music cassettes in Guangzhou (a linguistic market usually neglected by state-owned publishers) lend credence to this argument. Home taping has also been important in the dissemination of foreign pop music and indigenous Chinese rock left unrecorded by state companies.

The production of *tongsu* music cassettes, moreover, is indeed the sector of the industry most susceptible to the pressures of the "people's money," and content is consequently more loosely supervised by officials. The rush to capitalize on the cassette market has led to shoddy recording and manufacturing standards, and what writers in the official press like to describe as a flood of cassettes "pandering to the low tastes of the masses" with violent or sexual content.[44] Official calls for closer regulation of the cassette market have been implemented since June of 1989, in tandem with similar campaigns against publishers of pornographic and politically deviant books.[45] One consequence of this crackdown has been the removal of rock music cassettes from the marketplace.

Concerts are another volatile setting for the dissemination of *tongsu* music. As Pratt notes, large public gatherings contain within them both hegemonic and "emancipatory possibilities."[46] In urban areas, *tongsu* music concerts bring together groups of people numbering in the thousands (and often tens of thousands). These events are usually held in large, state-owned sports arenas, exhibition halls, auditoriums, and theaters. Most concerts are promoted by state-owned units.[47] The majority of *tongsu*

---

[43] Manuel, 6.

[44] Editors of *Yinyue yanjiu*, 27.

[45] Jin Zhaojun, "Shehui yinyue wenhua zai 1990" [Musical culture and society in 1990], *Gongren ribao*, January 1, 1990.

[46] Pratt, 11.

[47] In many municipalities, state-run "performance companies" (*yanchu gongsi*) are active in concert promotion. In addition, a limited number of private companies are involved in the promotion business. For an account of the private sector of the pop music economy, see Zhu Xingyi, Ge Guang, Qiao Guoliang, "Zou xue! Zou xue!".

music concerts are also singing contests. They follow a format, and involve musical styles and performance gestures, that are indistinguishable from their televised counterparts.[48] Audience participation is typically dampened by the presence of large numbers of police officers, who enforce rules prohibiting dancing, screaming, and the like.

Even so, emancipatory possibilities do indeed exist. The "Red Sorghum Chinese Country Rock and Roll" concert, a showcase of the "Northwest Wind" style in *tongsu* music organized by film director Zhang Yimou, is a case in point. Among the songs performed were disco versions of revolutionary songs like "Great Production" (*Da shengchan*).[49] These renditions veered towards overt parody, to the obvious delight of the youthful audience, and suggested an ironic re-appropriation of ideological territory long held sacred by the CCP.[50] The extent to which such moments of ironic pleasure can be characterized as emancipatory, however, remain ambiguous. As I will argue in the following chapter, rock concerts—whose role as a space for communal expressions of rebellion and emotional release has rendered them central to the life of the genre—are fraught with moments of similar ambiguity.

Talking About *Tongsu* Music, Talking About Rock

Thus far, my analysis of the ideological implications of the *tongsu* music genre has shuttled back and forth between investigations of what is produced(content) and how it is received (audience uses), between artifacts (music, lyrics, cassettes) and sensibilities (the attitudes of singers and songwriters). It is in the latter realm that the opposition between *tongsu* and rock music is often manifested most starkly. Songwriters' and singers' conceptions of *tongsu* music, while by no means entirely positive, substantially echoed many of the views aired in the press and critical

---

[48] Smaller-scale concerts, such as those held in neighborhood theaters, or provincial towns, often feature a single *gewutuan*. The format of these kind of shows stress variety: a pop song might be followed by acrobatics, or an exhibition of break-dancing.

[49] Kathryn Lowry, concert recording, Beijing, June 26, 1988.

[50] Kathryn Lowry, personal communication. The concert took place on June 26, 1988 at the Beijing Workers' Auditorium. Similar strategies have been adopted by rock musicians; Cui Jian's frenzied version of the revolutionary anthem "South Mud Bay" (*Nanniwan*) elicited the ire of the Beijing municipal officials, and led in part to his being banned from performing within city limits from 1986 to 1988. Another interesting permutation of the contemporary use of revolutionary songs came with the release of '*Dongfang hong' yaogun* ['East is red' rock], Zhongguo luyin luxiang chubanshe BB-48, 1988, performed by Jing Gangshan. Jing Gangshan denies that the tape's reworking of "The East is Red", the popular anthem of the Cultural Revolution, was either intentionally ironic, or representative of a longing for the verities of the recent past (*huigui yishi*).

discourse on the genre. Views on rock music, however, were revealing not only of the fact that there is indeed conflict between the two genres, but that critical divisions exist between the sensibilities of singers and songwriters within the *tongsu* genre itself. Songwriters expressed doubt and derision about the development of rock music, while singers consistently voiced their approval and admiration.

Critical discourse on popular music has been characterized by "conceptual chaos and theoretical weakness."[51] This fact is accounted for by the fact that such discourse has itself served as an arena for cultural struggle, for the battle to define what popular music is, and how it should be harnessed to the service of Chinese society. Such considerations, of course, must inevitably attempt to posit "authoritative definitions of social situations and legitimate interpretations of social needs."[52] Fan Weiqiang's article "Let Chinese Popular Music Go Towards the World," which I mentioned in the context of my discussion of the interaction of "River Elegy" and popular music, illustrates just such a process. In proposing that popular music overcome "the prescriptive power of traditional culture" or promote democratic political process through political satire, Fan issues an implicit attack on existing, hegemonic interpretations of social and cultural needs.[53] When the editors of *Music Research* (*Yinyue yanjiu*) attack commodified popular music for "pandering to the consumers' demands," they imply that mass culture should stand in a particular (and to my mind inevitably manipulative) sort of relation with its audiences.

The question I will now turn to is to what extent *tongsu* songwriters and singers have absorbed such ideologies. Songwriters, as a group, share the critic Jin Zhaojun's conviction that "musicology is inseparable from sociology," that *tongsu* music should be thought about primarily in terms of its social effects. Singers accept this interpretation of the social role of *tongsu* music, while expressing a detachment from the goals of would-be social engineers born of their disenfranchisement from the creation of *tongsu* music content. The comments of both singers and songwriters indicate an acceptance of a "top-down" approach to popular music. The "masses," in this model, are culturally illiterate, and need to be guided by the producers of mass culture, be it through moral, ideological, or aesthetic instruction. This basic understanding of the music as a simplified (*pujihua*) form that must cater to the masses in order to be accepted and

---

[51] Editors of *Yinyue yanjiu*, 17.
[52] Fraser, 6.
[53] Fan Weiqiang, 29.

understood (*bei laobaixing jieshou*) mimics exactly phrases habitually used in the official press in regard to *tongsu* music:

> *Tongsu* music is a simplified form of serious music, a compromise of quality that enables it to be accepted by the masses.[54]

> It's a form of art that's particularly easily accepted by the common people, and close to the common people.[55]

Statements like these were underlain by an undisguised contempt for the cultural level of the masses in question:

> They will appreciate simple songs, but when I'm performing, I sometimes feel like they just aren't getting the message. I like to sing relatively complex, difficult songs, but I have to sing songs they'll understand.[56]

> The quality and cultural level of the audience is really very low. At the "One Hundred Pop Stars" Concert, they were unenthusiastic when we sang really good material, but when we sang terrible songs, we got the warmest response.[57]

Only one singer, An Dong, believed that the audience's capacity for artistic discrimination had been underestimated by the government.

These convictions were voiced in the context of a general anxiety that *tongsu* music was not doing its job correctly. Echoing a spate of critical articles centering on this theme, singers and songwriters alike assailed the low quality of *tongsu* music production, and many of its institutional and economic problems (for instance, the lack of adequate copyright protection laws).[58] While their disdainful attitudes towards the audiences and condemnations of the state of *tongsu* music echoed themes prevalent in the official press, singers and songwriters generally apportioned the blame for these conditions on the institutions of *tongsu* music itself:

---

[54] Interview with Jing Gangshan.

[55] Interview with An Dong.

[56] Han and Jones, interview with Hu Yue.

[57] Interview with Jing Gangshan.

[58] Critical accounts of popular music in the press are common. Two prominent examples are Li Tianyi's "Tongsu yinyue heyuan luoru digu" [What caused popular music's decline?], *Renmin yinyue*, 1989/11; and Ma Dongfeng's "Lai ye congcong qu ye congcong: tongsu getan

If the audience had a greater capacity for judgement and higher standards, every level of the industry would improve. The problem can't be blamed on the common people but on songwriters and the Ministry of Culture, because they have the responsibility to provide the common people with guidance.[59]

Liu Huan proposed a more far-reaching explanation for the gulf separating singers from their audiences:

One reason is the commercialization of *tongsu* music. Another related reason is China's lack of social stability. There have been so many serious, rapid social changes, and it's hard to even describe the ways in which people have been oppressed. So even singers don't understand what they're doing, let alone understanding their audience.[60]

While *tongsu* music is seen as a "top-down" phenomena, rock was universally viewed as being "bottom-up," as a means for the expression of popular discontent. Even so, this view remained imbued with a characteristically low estimation of the rock audience:

One reason rock has become so popular with audiences is that it expresses a mood of defiance. It's not that the audience has really learned to appreciate or understand what rock is, but that it's an outlet for their feelings, a release.[61]

While this estimation of the social function of rock is shared by all interviewees, songwriters like Li Lifu questioned the very existence and legitimacy of rock music as a genre:

As for Cui Jian, he's not a rock musician, but a Chinese folk-style singer with a rock sensibility [*yaogun yishi*]. Rock is essentially a kind of emotional release, something that's out of step with society, a way to let off steam about oppression and depression. It's like a public toilet where people can express things they otherwise couldn't express. In the West, people have eaten their fill and have nothing to do, but still feel

xiankuang pouxi yu sikao" [Easy come, easy go: analysis and ideas on the current state of the popular music scene], *Yinyue shenghuo*, 1990/3, 4-6.

[59] Han and Jones, interview with Zhao Li and Wo Peng.

[60] Han and Jones, interview with Liu Huan and Li Lifu.

[61] Han and Jones, interview with Jing Gangshan.

dissatisfied, so they go out, listen to rock, get drunk, and jump around. They allow this to happen in the West, but we don't allow it here. Rock is anti-tradition, anti-morality, anti-logic. You can hear that in the lyrics. This is reasonable, but it isn't suitable under present conditions in China. Its development is not in tune with our national spirit. So Cui Jian is only representing a kind of ideology, but it isn't real rock. Real rock couldn't develop in China.[62]

Obviously, Li Lifu's contention that 'it couldn't happen here' would be hotly contested by musicians like Cui Jian, for whom the definition of "real rock" has less to do with musical style than with a "rock ideology" that enables its listeners "to feel real freedom."[63] Other songwriters, accepting both the existence of rock and a strictly extra-musical definition of its nature, criticize the music on the grounds of the narrow emotional parameters permitted by its rebellious ideology. Others object to rock musicians' narrow pursuit of form and fashion over substantive content. In response to the (factually incorrect) suggestion of one rock musician that rock musicians are generally better educated and more "cultured" than *tongsu* singers, another songwriter expressed the opinion (again, without basis in fact) that rock musicians are generally "idiots" and "problem youth" (*shehui qingnian*).[64] Such disputes clearly bespeak a certain degree of hostility and mutual opposition.

Tongsu singers, while echoing some of the complaints relating to the narrow emotional range of rock music, were far more sympathetic to rock musicians and their work. Even this failing, according to Jing Gangshan, could be attributed to the hostility of the government towards rock music:

> The government doesn't like rock music. As a consequence,
> the audience tends to see rock only in terms of the expression
> of anti-government feelings, not as something just to be
> enjoyed.[65]

This sympathetic understanding was underscored by the fact that singers' characterizations of rock music often tallied with those of rock musicians themselves:

---

[62] Han and Jones, interview with Li Lifu.

[63] Interview with Cui Jian.

[64] Han and Jones, interview with Jia Ding.

[65] Han and Jones, interview with Jing Gangshan.

Cui Jian's popularity is not due to the skill of his music or his band, but because he expresses inner feelings that are rarely expressed in China...Rock is definitely about oppression, about rebellion. It's very provocative, it wants to stir people up. Which isn't to say they want a *coup d'etat*...what matters is its truthfulness. Why is it that nowadays the only music that we can really respect is Cui Jian's music? It's because it's truthful. There are hardly any *tongsu* songs that are truthful.[66]

This kind of approbation led several of the singers to lament the absence of rock music from television:

Tongsu singers' ideas are different from the officials who run the TV programs. They don't like rock music, and won't let it on TV. Cui Jian and some other very good rock singers can't get on TV, and that prevents even more people from even knowing about their music. And we *tongsu* singers just don't have what it takes. I can't compare to someone like Cui Jian. I don't have his strength of character, his individualism. I can't tell them I won't go on TV unless I'm singing what I want to sing.[67]

Hu Yue, despite her grim portrayal of working in the *tongsu* music world, was quick to defend the necessity and viability of the genre, and chastised many of the younger rock musicians for "dressing up like foreign rock stars, thinking they're really cool, without really understanding society." Her succinct, idiosyncratic appraisal of the differences between rock and *tongsu* music merits citing at length:

I worship Cui Jian. He has depth, individuality, his own way of looking at things. His music is a cry; it's about being pressed down as far as you can be pressed, and then exploding out with a cry. I love to listen to this music, but I don't like to sing it. Maybe it's a question of personality. Maybe I still haven't been pushed down to that point. Maybe if I do get pushed down that far, I'll start crying out too. Then I'll sing rock too. If that happened, I wouldn't be able to sing love

---

[66] Han and Jones, interview with Zhao Li and Wo Peng.

[67] Han and Jones, interview with Hu Yue.

songs anymore. I'd open my mouth and nothing would come out—all I could do is scream.[68]

Hu Yue's reflections once again call to mind the experiences of Xiao Hu in "A Superfluous Story." If rock is a scream, Liu Suola suggests in an incident that takes place in the initial phases of Xiao Hu's search for moral authenticity, then *tongsu* music is like bumping one's head on the telephone pole of the mundane:

> On Monday, I was hurrying to catch a bus to get to work when I hit my head on a telephone pole. Since I was looking back at the bus and running forward when I hit it, I was completely defenseless. There was a violent bang that sounded as if I'd hit a bell. The "chop suey" in my head shifted position, I bounced back several feet, and just as I opened my mouth to let out a string of screams and curses to the street, the breath in my throat shaped itself into, "I'm sorry, thank you, bye-bye."[69]

---

[68] Ibid.
[69] Liu Suola, 111.

Tongsu singer Hu Yue

Tongsu singer An Dong

March 1990 cover of *University Students* featuring Cui Jian's Asian Games tour

Punk Rocker He Yong, 1990 (Michael Rice)

Dou Wei of the Black Panthers [*Heibao*], 1990 (Michael Rice)

Zhu Xiaomin performing with his Tutu Band, 1990 (Michael Rice)

4

ROCK MUSIC AS A GENRE

Rock musicians sing songs that don't have
government approval. Tongsu singers sing songs
that do.

—Jing Gangshan

Tongsu is the music made by people in the song and
dance troupes. Rock is made by independent
musicians.

—Dong Dong, rock musician

The basic role of Cui Jian's band and rock in general
is to express discontent.

—Liu Xiaosong, rock
musician

In the preceding chapter, I showed how cultural hegemony in
tongsu music is partly enforced through institutional curbs on the
subjectivity of *tongsu* singers. *Tongsu* singers are divested of control over
their songs, their voices, even their bodies. I argue here that what places
rock in opposition to *tongsu* music, indeed what makes rock "rock," is its
self-conscious reclamation of a subjective voice. The central concern of
rock musicians, their fans (and often their critics) lies in the genre's capacity
for authentic self-expression (*ziwo biaoxian*) and emotional release (*xuanxie*)
in the face of oppression (*yayi*), be it political or cultural.

This rebellious sensibility has forced rock music to develop
underground, outside of both the institutions of *tongsu* music, and the
public sphere through which it is disseminated. I begin this chapter by
briefly recounting the development of rock music and its oppositional
subcultural milieu. The bulk of the chapter, though, is devoted to an

analysis of the distinctive ways in which musicians working within the rock scene go about making and performing their music. I approach the accounts of the rock music genre provided by interviews with rock musicians with an eye towards answering the same set of questions I raised in the preceding chapter. How is the music made? Who controls its content? How is it performed? How do rock concerts reflect rock sensibilities? How do rock musicians evaluate themselves, and where do they place themselves in relation to *tongsu* music? In each case, the answers to these questions underscore the fundamental divergences of rock music from *tongsu* music. Finally, I argue that the way in which rock is produced and performed creates the potentiality for both 'negotiated' and 'emancipatory' uses of the music.

The Development of a Rock Music Underground

Before I provide a view of the distinctive practices and sensibilities that characterized Chinese rock music in the summer of 1990, it is important to review the brief history of rock's development in China. Rock music is an underground phenomenon. Its development took place outside of the institutional structures of *tongsu* music, and was spurred along only through the aid of private entrepreneurs, college students, and the musical and financial support of foreigners residing in Beijing. This fact is responsible for several of the genre's most salient features. First, its musicians are amateurs; lacking affiliation with state-run production units, they have been compelled to write, rehearse, and record their music through unofficial channels. Second, rock performances are never televised, and only rarely take place in large state-owned auditoriums. Instead, privately financed rock 'parties' are relegated to the margins of urban life, to bars, restaurants, and college cafeterias. Third, the CCP's exclusion of rock from the legitimacy of the public sphere has profoundly colored the perception (held by musicians, fans, and critics alike) that rock is essentially a subversive, rebellious form of expression.

Finally, as the following pages will make clear, the four-year history of Chinese rock music must be seen in the context of larger cultural and political struggles. The degree to which the CCP has either damned or praised this new genre has varied in direct relation to the prevailing political climate. During periods of relative ideological relaxation (for instance, the summer of 1988), CCP officials have been willing to allow rock to reach wide audiences by way of the print media and large-scale concerts. Conversely, when the CCP has narrowed the limits of acceptable cultural expression (as in the 1987 Anti-Bourgeois Liberalization Campaign, or following the suppression of the student movement in 1989), rock music has been one of the first forms of popular culture to be restricted.

Rock's increasing marginalization, though, should not be seen as having limited its ideological force, its influence in the lives of its listeners. Indeed, that influence has often been amplified through the genre's frequent infiltrations of the mass media, through the presence of a subcultural form in public spheres generally reserved for the products of state mass culture. The interrelations between these different spheres, and rock's affinities with an intermediary youth culture centered around college students, is the subject of the final chapter of the book.

The development of rock in China is in many ways the story of its most innovative and popular figure, Cui Jian. Originally a trumpeter in the Beijing Philharmonic Orchestra (*Beijing jiaoxiang yuetuan*), Cui Jian began to compose his own songs in 1984. In 1985, he formed his own band, the Building Blocks (*Qiheban*, after a traditional wooden puzzle with seven pieces), with six colleagues from the orchestra.[1] At the same time, a small group of like-minded musicians and art students (including Wang Di and Sun Guoqing, who went on to fame as "rock-style" singers within the *tongsu* framework) established their own band, the Weebles (*Budaoweng*, referring to a traditional Chinese toy that wobbles but won't fall down). These early efforts were characterized by financial and logistical difficulties. Neither group had enough money to buy new instruments, rent rehearsal space, or arrange for performances. The fact that rock music was as yet virtually unheard of in China, and thus ideologically suspect, eliminated the possibility of official institutional support. Instead, rock musicians began to rely on the financial assistance of private companies in Beijing and Shenzhen, and the tutelage in rock music techniques provided by foreign students in Beijing.[2] College campuses, in turn, provided Cui Jian with a forum for his music: his first public performance with his ADO band (which featured a Madagascaran guitarist and a Hungarian guitarist) took place at Beijing University.

On May 10th, 1986, this burgeoning underground rock subculture was first exposed to mainstream audiences when Cui Jian performed his "I Have Nothing" at the annual "One Hundred Pop Stars" (*Baiming gexing*)

---

[1] The early efforts of this group can be heard on Cui Jian, *Langzi gui* [The wanderer returns], BMG Pacific/Current 8.28031, 1989.

[2] For a history of these early attempts at establishing rock music in China, see Han Xiaohui, "Sun Guoqing jianying" [Sun Guoqing: a sketch], and Wang Zhi, "Huajia gexing: ji yaogun yueshou Wang Di de chengzhang" [Painter/pop star: a record of rock singer Wang Di's development], in Wang Yanqi and Han Xiaohui.

concert at the Beijing Worker's Stadium. According to one account, the incongruity of his battered PLA khakis, unconventional stage manner, and rough vocal delivery reduced an audience of nearly twenty-thousand pop fans to stunned silence. Within minutes, however, the novelty and emotional intensity of his performance began to elicit wild cheers and frenzied dancing: "a new chapter in the history of Chinese popular music had begun."[3] Within days, Cui Jian had become the talk of Beijing. Within weeks, news and unauthorized recordings of "I Have Nothing" had reached cities thousands of miles away from Beijing.[4] In the following months, Cui Jian performed at several other large-scale concerts, and his fame grew steadily.

In 1987, however, Cui became a victim of the CCP's "Anti-Bourgeois Liberalization Campaign" (*Fandui zichan jieji ziyouhua*). He provoked the ire of both Beijing municipal officials and his own work unit by performing a rock version of the revolutionary song, "Southern Muddy Bay" (*Nanniwan*). According to several reports, a high ranking CCP official couched his subsequent decision to ban Cui Jian from performing in these words, "How could a young person in new socialist China have nothing?"[5] In May of 1987, he was fired by the Beijing Philharmonic Orchestra, banned from performing at large-scale concerts and appearing on television, and prevented from recording "I Have Nothing." Ironically, the song's popularity continued undiminished, and it was recorded by several mainstream singers, including Liu Huan and Sun Guoqing. In short, Cui Jian was ejected from participation in the *tongsu* music industry and its public sphere.

Cui continued to perform in the context of Beijing's underground rock scene. Venues included a foreign-owned restaurant, Maxim's, and several university campuses. In the summer of 1988, as reformers in the CCP once again gained the upper hand, restrictions were loosened, and the *People's Daily* (a CCP organ comparable to the former Soviet Union's *Pravda*) published an article praising Cui, and expressing the hope that in the future he would not be subject to any more "unfair treatment."[6] Soon

---

[3] Xiao Feng, 1.

[4] Ping Fang and Ma Mu, "'Yiwu suoyou,' yaogun yu touji: wei yayunhui juankuan yibaiwan yuan yiyan jishi" ["I have nothing", rock and opportunism: a record of the tour to raise one million *yuan* for the Asian Games], *Xiju shijie*, 1990/ 3-4, 3.

[5] Bai Jieming, "Yaogun fanshen le" [Has rock stood up?], *Jiushi niandai*, 1988/11, 94.

[6] Gu Tu, "Cong 'Yiwu suoyou' shuodao yaogunyue: Cui Jian de zuopin weishenme shou huanying" [From "I have nothing" to rock music: why have Cui Jian's works become popular?], *Renmin ribao*, July 16, 1988. Gu Tu's contention that the appraisal of Cui Jian's music (or any art form, for that matter) should not be linked to "social considerations or class struggle" was remarkably liberal in its disavowal of the dominant critical paradigm that has prevailed in China since 1949.

after, Cui was offered a recording contract by a state-owned unit, China Tourism Audio-Visual Publishers (*Zhongguo luyou luxiang chubanshe*). He spent nearly a year recording his first album, *New Long March Rock* (*Xin changzheng lushang de yaogun*), with the aid of an American producer, Kenny Bloom.[7] In March 1989, one month before the outbreak of the democracy movement, Cui Jian performed two concerts at the Beijing Exhibition Hall coinciding with the release of his new album. Black market ticket prices escalated to one hundred *yuan* (U.S. $ 30, or roughly a month's salary) by the night of the show, indicating Cui Jian's continuing popularity among Beijing's youth, despite his long absence from (and only fleeting presence in) the public sphere.

The democracy movement had several important consequences for the development of rock music. First, rock music and rock musicians played an active role in the movement. Cui Jian performed for students in Tiananmen Square, and his *New Long March Rock* album became an integral part of the "soundtrack" of the movement in a manner reminiscent of the relationship between rock and the American counter-culture of the late 1960's:

> ...music was heard all over the square. Two of the most popular singers were Qi Qin [a Taiwanese rock singer] and Cui Jian, the John Lennon of China. As I walked around, I saw couples arm in arm, and the boy was often singing one of Cui Jian's songs to the girl, "I was looking at you very closely, and this made me feel so good that I forgot I was without a home."[8]

---

[7] Bloom has started his own production company, KB Communications, in order to promote Wei Hua's *The Sun Rises* in Hong Kong and Taiwan. Bloom also acted as the recording engineer for Cui Jian's latest album, *Jiejue* [Solution], EMI FX-500762, 1991. China Tourism Audio-Visual Publishers is perhaps the only state-run unit that has made a concerted effort to record rock music. In addition to Cui's *New Long March Rock*, they released a collection of *tongsu* singers (including Wang Di, Tian Zhen, Liu Huan, Sun Guoqing, and Cui himself) performing original compositions with Cui's ADO band. See *Jin mu shui huo tu: Zhongguo wu da yaogun chenxing* [Gold, wood, water, fire, earth: China's five greatest rock stars], Zhongguo luyou luxiang chubanshe, 1989. This time span was highly unusual given that most *tongsu* records are recorded in the space of two or three days. Interview with Liu Xiaosong, Beijing, June 20, 1990.

[8] Shen Tong, *Almost A Revolution*, (Boston: Houghton Mifflin, 1990), 310. The line is taken from one of Cui Jian's most powerful songs, "Yikuai hongbu" [A piece of red cloth], which is discussed in detail in chapter five.

Other rock musicians participated more actively in the movement, and at least one was detained (and subsequently released) for having thrown Molotov cocktails at PLA vehicles on the night of June 4, 1989.[9]

Finally, the movement brought mainland rock to the attention of Hong Kong and Taiwanese investors. Cui Jian's *New Long March Rock* was released in Hong Kong and Taiwan by EMI records, and "I Have Nothing" became a rallying cry of the democracy movement in Hong Kong.[10] In the wake of the crackdown, rock musicians in Beijing have become increasingly reliant on foreign investment and promotion, often through the very same record companies (EMI, RCA) that dominated the "yellow music" market in the 1920's and 1930's.[11]

In the first six months of 1990, the rock subculture centered in Beijing underwent several important changes. First and foremost, the number of rock bands rehearsing and performing in Beijing increased exponentially. In 1988, the city had at most three active groups. By the summer of 1990, that figure had increased to thirty. This proliferation of bands brought a new diversity of rock styles, including bands exclusively devoted to heavy metal and punk rock. Bars and restaurants around the city began to regularly feature weekly rock parties where up to five bands performed to other rock musicians, rock fans, students, and *getihu*. This new crop of rock bands was first exposed to a wider audience in February 1990 at the "Modern Music Festival" held at Beijing's Capital Auditorium (*Shoudu Tiyuguan*). The concert, organized by the lead singer of the Breathing Band, Wei Hua, and sponsored by the Performance Department of the privately owned China Arts Exchange Company (*Zhongguo yishu jiaoliu gongsi*), featured six bands (including the Breathing Band, ADO, 1989, Tang Dynasty Band, Cobra, and Circumstances).[12]

The freedom to hold such an event, of course, remains provisional. In the months following the "Modern Music Festival," the boundaries of acceptable have narrowed once more, and rock has been barred from participation in even the kind of limited 'public sphere' constituted by large-scale concerts. As I mentioned in the introduction, Cui Jian's national tour

---

[9] Interview with Liu Xiaosong, June 23, 1990. The musician in question was not Liu himself.

[10] The record was released as *Yiwu suoyou* [I have nothing], EMI Hong Kong CDFH-50037, 1989.

[11] In 1990, two rock records barred from release in the mainland have been released by foreign companies in Hong Kong. They are Wei Hua's *Taiyang sheng* [The sun rises], BMG Pacific 8.280048, 1990, and Chang Kuan's *Chongxin jihua xianzai* [Making plans for now], EMI FH-500784, 1990.

[12] 36,000 people attended the event. See Tong Wei, 18-21.

to raise funds for the Asian Games was cancelled in mid-career in April 1990. In the fall of 1990, he was prohibited from performing at Beijing University. Because rock parties in Chinese-owned venues have been subject to police harassment, musicians have increasingly been compelled to hold events in foreign-run restaurants in Beijing, where there is some measure of "extra-territoriality." The release of two rock recordings (Wei Hua's *The Sun Rises*, and Chang Kuan's *Making Plans For Now*) have been banned in the mainland by the Ministry of Culture.[13] Cui Jian's latest album, *Solution*, was released in the mainland only after months of negotiations and bureaucratic foot-dragging.[14] Despite its frequent penetration of the public sphere, rock music has been increasingly pushed into the margins, into reliance on foreign support, and subcultural forms of resistance.

Making Rock Music: The Poetics of Authenticity

> This guitar in my hands is like a knife...
> I want to cut at your hypocrisy till I see some truth [15]

In contrast to *tongsu* singers, rock musicians write their own songs. Rock music's central figures are not its singers and songwriters, but its *singer-songwriters*. Its basic personnel unit is not the *gewutuan*, but the rock band (*yaogun yuedui*). In terms of structure and instrumentation, Chinese rock bands do not differ significantly from their Western counterparts. Lead singers—who tend to write much of the band's material, and command much of the audience's attention—double on electric guitar. The typical group's sound is completed with the addition of an additional guitarist, a keyboard player, a bassist, a drummer, and various other instrumentalists.[16] All of the band's musicians usually collaborate in composing new songs.

Who, then, are these musicians? What are their backgrounds? The information I gathered through a series of formal and informal interviews over the course of the summer of 1990 yields surprisingly few commonalities that might facilitate generalization. The ages, occupational,

---

[13] Dan Southerland, personal communication, Harvard University, January 31, 1990.

[14] The lyrics of two of its most controversial songs, "Like a Knife" and "The Last Gunshot" are conspicuously absent from the lyric sheet of the mainland release of the album.

[15] Cui Jian, "Xiang yiba daozi" [Like a knife], music and lyrics by Cui Jian. A recording is included on his album *Jiejue*.

[16] Cui Jian's ADO band, for instance, included Liu Yuan, who played the saxophone, the *dizi*, and *suona*. Cui Jian himself often plays trumpet with his new band.

range from 16 to 33 years old. There are college graduates and high school drop-outs, conservatory trained musicians as well as teenagers who taught themselves how to play guitar. A significant minority abandoned careers in *tongsu* music in order to pursue careers in rock music; others are simply high school drop-outs or unemployed youth.[17]

I will focus this discussion on a group of five interviewees: Cui Jian, Liu Xiaosong, Zhu Xiaomin, Dong Dong, and Gao Qi.[18] Two of the five have undergone formal musical training. Cui Jian, of course, began his musical career in the Beijing Philharmonic Orchestra; Liu Xiaosong (Cui Jian's current drummer) spent seven years studying traditional Chinese percussion, and worked for five years with the Beijing Opera Company. Three of the five worked within the *tongsu* framework before joining rock bands. Zhu Xiaomin, whose father composes regional folk opera, was a worker in an audiocassette manufacturing factory for several years, and later acted as an editor at an audio-visual publishing unit. In April 1990, he formed the Tutu Band. Dong Dong left a job as a keyboard player at the Beijing Song and Dance Troupe, and presently plays in both the Breathing and Tutu bands. Liu Xiaosong often participated in *tongsu* recording sessions as a free-lance musician before joining Cui Jian's band. Gao Qi, although his father is a choral conductor, learned guitar on his own, and dropped out of the China Institute of Tourism (*Zhongguo luyou xueyuan*) in his third year in order to play guitar and write songs for the Breathing Band.

Rock musicians, *by definition*, are amateur musicians; in the eyes of the state they are "unemployed." Rock musicians neither work for a nationalized work unit nor register themselves officially as private entrepreneurs (unlike *tongsu* singers who choose to leave their troupes and "go to the cave"). This lack of institutional affiliation remains highly unusual in a society where well over ninety percent of workers are employed by the state.[19] In this context, severing oneself from the lifetime job security (the "iron rice bowl") provided by a work unit is no easy matter, either financially or psychologically. Cui Jian's comments on his decision to devote himself to rock music indicate the extent to which such a move constituted a radical break with his own past, and with orthodox ways of

---

[17] These observations are by no means intended as accurate assessments of rock demographics. They are based upon interviews and informal discussions with some thirty participants in the rock scene in Beijing.

[18] Again, this group does not constitute a representative sample. Instead, I have chosen to focus on these five musicians because they provided me with the most revealing and comprehensive interview material.

[19] Gold, 177.

making popular music in China: "I worked hard, said farewell to my old life, and started a new life from zero."[20] Other interviewees described leaving their work units in terms of their overriding passion for rock music:

> I was working as a music editor, but when rock became my main interest, I just had to leave.[21]

> In my first two years of college, I taught myself guitar and songwriting. By my third year, all I wanted to do was write songs. I felt a huge conflict between my music and my education, so I dropped out and devoted myself to the music. Generally speaking, everyone who plays rock music went through a similar process...the fact is that a lot of these people used to do *tongsu* music, but couldn't bear to go on playing such lousy songs. Playing rock is much more joyful, much more satisfying.[22]

Even so, abandoning the financial support and facilities of a song and dance troupe makes the production of rock music that much more difficult. Electric guitars, recording equipment, and amplifiers are expensive and scarce. Rehearsal space is nearly impossible to find. The cost of independently renting a recording studio (1000 *yuan* , or roughly $400 U.S., per day) is prohibitive. Rock musicians are thus forced to subsist on their own earnings:

> We're just like underground rock musicians in the West. We have to rely on ourselves, because none of us have work units. We make enough from rock parties to afford basic necessities and rehearsal space. There's no comparison between the incomes of rock musicians and *tongsu* singers. That's why most *tongsu* singers can't understand what playing rock is all about.[23]

The great majority of rock music is rehearsed (and often recorded on portable four-track recorders) either at home or in rented rooms.[24]

---

[20] Xiao Feng, 2.

[21] Interview with Zhu Xiaomin, Beijing, July 19, 1990.

[22] Interview with Gao Qi, Beijing, July 20, 1990.

[23] Interview with Zhu Xiaomin.

[24] The Women's Band (*Nuzidui*), for instance, got their start with the help of the owner of a music shop that lent them instruments and rehearsal space. Tong Wei, 19. As Gao Qi points

At the same time, the paucity of resources available to rock musicians has led many bands to turn to foreign investors for aid:

> You can't buy Fender and Gibson guitars in Beijing. And rehearsal space is extremely difficult to find. If you practice in an apartment, the neighbors can't take the noise, and they react really badly. Because of these kinds of problems, a band like Black Panthers went ahead and got financial backing from Taiwanese investors.[25]

Zhu Xiaomin likens this phenomenon to China's "open-door policy" of encouraging foreign investment over the past decade:

> China is a poor country, and it needs capital investment to develop its industries, to construct a modern infrastructure. The same goes for music...we need foreign capital for our basic musical infrastructure.[26]

The financial support of multinational recording companies operating out of Hong Kong and Taiwan has become especially critical in the recording and promotion of rock records. The recording costs of Cui Jian's second album, *Solution*, were shared by Cui himself and a Taiwanese company, Rock Record and Tape (*Yaoshi changpian*). Both Wei Hua and Chang Kuan have had albums released outside of the P.R.C. on foreign labels.

These travails, of course, are borne precisely because they allow rock musicians to escape the strictures of the *tongsu* music industry, to sing their own songs. This freedom, of course, is a double-edged sword; in being excluded from the *tongsu* apparatus, rock is hidden from the view of the majority of China's popular music audience. Because of this marginalization, making rock music is far simpler than producing *tongsu* music. Singer and songwriter are embodied in the same person. Rock singers are not required to sing songs penned by the "Northern Monopoly." Their activities are neither monitored, nor financially exploited by a work unit. The rock songwriter need not heed the demands of the propaganda chief ("write a song that will represent young people"), or submit his work to a censor before recording. Nor will she be asked to sing a propaganda

---

out, even these makeshift conditions are vastly better than those faced by would-be rock musicians in provincial towns and rural areas, who "make their own drums and guitars out of boxes and wire." Interview with Gao Qi.

[25] Interview with Dong Dong, Beijing, June 21, 1990.

[26] Interview with Zhu Xiaomin.

song, cut her hair, or wear certain clothes for a concert or television appearance. Finally, and rather ironically, the rock musician is free from many of the demands imposed on *tongsu* songwriters by the market, by the need to "serve the people's money." The rock singer—and this claim lies at the heart of the self-proclaimed rock sensibility—is free to sing herself, to convey her deepest, most authentic feelings.

How does this sensibility inform what kinds of songs are written? What kind of content emerges from the ironic freedom conferred on rock songwriters by their marginalization? The preoccupation with authentic self-expression underlying the vast majority of rock lyrics precludes the possibility of straightforwardly hegemonic content. Rock lyricists self-consciously concern themselves with the emancipation of the individual in the face of oppression: propaganda songs along the lines of "The Valiant Spirit of Asia" are simply beside the point. Even so, rock lyrics display a *uniformity* of tone and content that suggests that songs of individual authenticity are used both as a means of emotional release, and as a medium through which the rock subculture coheres as group united in opposition to the society in which they are embedded.

Released from the restrictions of the *tongsu* music scene, rock songwriters have produced a body of work remarkable for its lack of thematic diversity. Most of the conventional song types that constantly recur in *tongsu* music—songs in praise of the motherland, socialism, or one's native place (*zange, xianglian ge*), 'modernized' folk songs (*minge*), and love songs (*shuqing gequ*) are entirely absent. Instead, rock lyrics are set in a colloquial, urban idiom, and treat themes of alienation, oppression and the desire for emotional release. As James Scott argues, such a lack of variety may well be a product of the fact that dissident subcultures not only provide a space for the expression of discontent, but "serve to discipline as well as to formulate patterns of resistance."[27] Thus, "sentiments that are idiosyncratic, unrepresentative, or have only weak resonance within the group are likely to be selected against or censored."[28] The resonance of the serious, subjective explorations of urban Chinese life that are selected reflect a conscious reaction to the "emptiness" of *tongsu* music (as well as the "frivolity" of much Western rock and roll):

> The fame of the songwriters who control the industry is due to their connections with officials. They are a conservative

[27] Scott, 118.
[28] Scott, 119.

monopoly, and their music is basically just popularized folk songs [*liuxinghua de minge*]. So there's obviously antagonism between rock and *tongsu*. 80% of the pop songs are about love. Even heavy metal bands like Tang Dynasty and Black Panthers aren't that empty, though they might look like they're just superficially stylish with their long hair. Neither of those bands have imitated American heavy metal. They sing about real life, life in China, not sex and drugs.[29]

For rock lyricists, "life in China" comes uncannily close to mimicking the world described in Liu Suola's "A Superfluous Story." Rock lyrics—taken as a whole—obsessively recount a kind of archetypical narrative not unlike Xiao Hu's own search for moral authenticity in a world shot through with hypocrisy.[30] The thematic and narrative center of the rock lyric is invariably the moment in which a breakthrough to moral authenticity is achieved. The singer confronts the past and discovers only oppression (*yayi*), hypocrisy (*xuwei*), and alienation. The singer resolves to cast off this burdensome legacy, to forge a new world of freedom and authenticity. Cui Jian's "Won't Cover It up Again" (*Bu zai yanshi*) is a typical example of this process of self-discovery and moral self-definition:

> My tears won't be for weeping anymore
> My smile won't be play-acting again
> Your freedom belongs to heaven and earth
> Your courage belongs to you
>
> I've got no money, got no place, just have the past
> I've said a lot, thought a lot, and I have less and less of an idea
> I'm not pitiful, and I'm not hateful, because I'm not you
> I understand abandonment, and understand irresponsibility
> But I've got no way to leave
>
> ...My endurance won't be put to hard labor again
> My sincerity won't be paid in tears anymore
> My strength won't be in hypocrisy again
> My tenderness won't be repented anymore

---

[29] Interview with Dong Dong, Beijing, July 11, 1990.

[30] Only one rock singer, He Yong, writes lyrics that diverge significantly from this pattern. While still treating themes of oppression and alienation, He Yong's imagery is far more violent that that of the majority of rock lyricists. See chapter five for a discussion of his song "Lajichang" [Garbage dump].

...My freedom belongs to heaven and earth
My courage belongs to me[31]

The oppression and untruth from which the singer wishes to be liberated are described in term of emotional blockage, of alienation from the self and from others, as in the Tutu Band's "Can't Find Any Feeling" (*Shenme ye juebuchu*):

I don't know if I've forgotten happiness
Or if happiness has forgotten me
Suffering people in a world of suffering
Can't find any feeling

I don't know if I've forgotten love
Or if love has forgotten me
Unloved people in a world of people not worth loving
Can't find any feeling

I don't know if I've forgotten ideals
Or if ideals have forgotten me
Blind people in a blind black night
Can't find any feeling...[32]

Cui Jian's "Let Me Go Wild In This Snowy Place" (*Kuai rang wo zai zhe xuedi shang sa dian ye*) is another variant on this theme:

I bared my shoulders to meet the snow and wind
I ran down the road out of the hospital
Don't block my way, I don't want any clothes
Because my disease is that I have no feeling

...Give me some excitement, doctor
Give me a little love, nurse
Let me cry or let me laugh

[31] Cui Jian, "Bu zai yanshi" [Won't cover it up again] , music and lyrics by Cui Jian. On Cui Jian, *Xin changzheng lushang de yaogun* [New long march rock].
[32] Tutu Band, "Shenme ye juebuchu" [Can't find any feeling], music by Zhu Xiaomin, lyrics by Da Ta. Live recording, Ritan Park, Beijing, July 7, 1990.

Let me go wild in this snowy place...[33]

Alienation, in turn, springs from a deep sense of isolation from the public world and its normative activities and pleasures—commerce, urban street life, and often, *tongsu* music:

> Sitting all alone at the side of road
> Looking at the cars come and go
> Inside the store the pop songs sound bright
> But I'm hearing desolation[34]

Often, the rock singer depicts himself as the focus of active public disapproval and public humiliation. An anonymous public eye bears down upon the freedom and sheer physical exuberance of the rock musician's unorthodox lifestyle:

> Right next to us are observing eyes
> Every action, every move is caught in their staring eyes
> When I'm yelling, when I'm dancing, when I'm smiling at a girl
> Look behind me, there's someone saying my lifestyle's bad...[35]

This kind of constant surveillance is, of course, not merely a metaphor, but a fact of Chinese life. Work units encourage colleagues to report to the authorities on each other's ideological deviations. University students are required to write obligatory "self-criticisms" for infractions as seemingly minor as playing mah-jong. Neighborhood and street committees oversee the conduct of residents living under their jurisdiction. Rock musicians see the trespassing of the collective into personal space as a primary nemesis:

> The feudal power of society is against rock music. Feudal
> power comes from blind obedience to traditional Confucian
> relationships, to hierarchy. The tightness of our social circles
> is a good example. The group won't let the individual alone.
> Even the way we Chinese say hello is feudal. Instead of just
> greeting somebody, we invade their privacy: "Where are you

---

[33] Cui Jian, "Kuai rang wo zai zhe xuedi shang sa dian ye" [Let me go wild in this snowy place], music and lyrics by Cui Jian. Released on Cui Jian, *Jiejue*.

[34] Breathing Band, "Wo bu zai mang" [I'm not busy anymore], music by Cao Jun, lyrics by Wei Hua. Released on Wei Hua, *Taiyang sheng*.

[35] Chang Kuan, "Zuofeng buhao" [Bad lifestyle], music and lyrics by Chang Kuan. On *Chongxin jihua xianzai*.

going?" or "Have you eaten yet?" The government is feudal, too...[36]

These incursions afflict the rock singer with a pervasive sense of physical and spiritual violation:

> I never dared to turn myself around
> I never dared to stand up
> *I sensed the iciness of all those eyes early on*
> Now I feel a powerful hope, I want to hover in the sky
> But I don't know where I can head, where I can go to fly
>
> I want to know what it is
> What is a truthful life
> I want to clear up this illusion
> I want to look around in every direction
> *My throat's been strangled*, but I'm thirsting to sing
> But I don't know where I can go to hear an echo
>
> *All of the gloomy eyes are staring hard at me*
> *All of the icy hands are touching me*
> *All those silent thoughts are surrounding me*
> But I only need you to come answer me...[37]

At this point, in Hu Yue's words, the singer cannot help but to "explode out with a cry," to "scream." A sense of physical violation—echoing that expressed by *tongsu* singers—can only be dispelled through angry, idealistic assertions of the singer's own freedom. In "A Superfluous Story," Xiao Hu's revulsion for the Propaganda Chief's grasping hands and obscene eyes erupts into a song that condemns his corruption and hypocrisy through the use of idealized abstractions: "youth," "purity," and authenticity. Wei Hua, armed with a similar battery of idealized qualities (freedom, truth, lies, promises) against an unnamed adversary, sings the following lyric at a rock party in an analogous act of defiance:

---

[36] Interview with Dong Dong. Interestingly, Dong Dong's statements here substantially echo the ideas of the German sociological Georg Simmel, who in an essay entitled "Group Expansion and the Development of Individuality" comments that, "feudalism generated nothing but narrow circles that bound individual to individual and restricted each by his obligation to the other." Georg Simmel, trans. Donald N. Levine, *On Individuality and Social Forms*, (Chicago: University of Chicago Press, 1971), 270.

[37] Italics mine. The suppression of individuality is consistently figured in physical terms. Breathing Band, "Huilai" [Return], music and lyrics by Gao Qi, on Wei Hua, *Taiyang sheng* [The sun rises].

Don't try to stop me again
Don't use lies to trick me
Don't try to hide the truth from me again
I'll struggle free of these bonds in the end
I don't need your promises, time would drag by slowly
Even if I've suffered, the sun's rays will shine on me in the end[38]

The Czech playwright Vaclav Havel—who is of course no stranger to the mechanics of Communist hegemony—illumines what is at stake in this eruption of alienated private sensibilities back into the public world:

> [Official ideology] consequently merges with reality. A general and all-embracing lie begins to predominate; people begin adapting to it, and everyone in some part of their lives compromises with the lie or coexists with it. Under these conditions, *to assert the truth, to behave authentically by breaking through the all-englobing web of lies*—in spite of everything, including the risk that one might find oneself up against the whole world—is an act of extraordinary political importance.[39]

Ultimately, the poetics of authenticity have more to do with collectivity than individuality. As Havel's comments make clear, the emancipatory impact of rock lyrics is contingent upon publicity, on performance. Self-realization is a lonely business. Authenticity of itself is insufficient. Wei Hua, having embarked upon a search for a "truthful existence," longs for someone who will listen, for somewhere she can "hear an echo" of her song. The singer needs to reach a community of fellow sufferers, a community that defines itself by its common opposition to the larger public world. As James C. Scott notes in his *Domination and the Arts of Resistance:*

> Within this social circle the subordinate is afforded a partial refuge from the humiliations of domination, and it is from this circle that the audience (one might say "the public") for the hidden transcript [i.e., the ideology of resistance] is drawn. Suffering from the same humiliations or, worse, subject to the

---

[38] Breathing Band, "Bie zai shitu zulan wo" [Don't try to stop me again], music by Gao Qi, lyrics by Wei Hua and Gao Qi. Live recording, June 16, 1990. Also on Wei Hua, *Taiyang sheng* [The sun rises].

[39] Italics mine. Vaclav Havel, as cited in Scott, 206.

same terms of subordination, they have a shared interest in jointly creating a discourse of dignity, of negation, and of justice. They have, in addition, a shared interest in concealing a social site apart from domination where such a hidden transcript can be elaborated in comparative safety.[40]

I argue in the next section that the rock "party" is just such a site, that it is only in the context of *performance* that rock musicians and fans band together in a common ritual of release and resistance.

Performing Rock Music

Rock performances are fundamentally different from the televised singing contests I reviewed in the preceding chapter. Where singing contests and *tongsu* concerts are organized through official CCP channels, rock parties are promoted by private entrepreneurs. *Tongsu* performances take place on television, and in officially sanctioned public spaces (state-owned theaters and stadiums). Rock parties are held in bars, and foreign-owned restaurants. *Tongsu* performances feature a succession of singers backed by one band; rock parties feature several different rock bands. *Tongsu* concerts are distinguished by heavy police supervision and strictures against drinking alcohol, dancing, and yelling. At rock parties, such activities are the rule rather than the exception. *Tongsu* singers perform their songs using a series of rigidly formulaic gestures, while the behavior and clothing styles adopted by rock musicians are calculated to convey authenticity. Finally, I argue here that the very musical idiom through which the rock sensibility is communicated to its audiences at rock parties is exactly tailored to effect the affective release from oppression which constitutes these events' principal end.

How, then, does the rock subculture set about "carving out for itself social spaces insulated from control and surveillance from above"?[41] Insulation, of course, hinges on a measure of exclusivity. Rock parties are organized through an unofficial network of musicians, and private entrepreneurs:

> Parties aren't organized through any fixed channels. They're organized casually. Bands can play if they want, and if they don't that's all right, too. Usually someone contacts a

---

[40] Scott, 114.
[41] Scott, 118.

restaurant or bar, and then arranges the show with the bands. It usually isn't the owners of the venue who arrange things, but a private entrepreneur. This kind of party is a new phenomenon in China, so there's no formal procedure for anything, no system. Each band member earns next to nothing from the parties, and that's how we support ourselves.[42]

Such parties, moreover, are not openly promoted or advertised. News of an event is passed through an informal network of those "in the know"; unobtrusive flyers are posted on college campuses. Tickets are usually sold by enterprising college students and the musicians themselves in advance of the night of the show, effectively excluding those without prior knowledge of the event. The very price of the tickets—from 25 to 30 *yuan*, or one-third of the average worker's monthly wage—tends to bar all but foreign students, wealthy private entrepreneurs, and those close enough to the musicians to be admitted without charge (a group that includes college students and artists).

The venues in which rock parties are held also reflect an effort to insulate these gatherings from control and surveillance. Parties are usually held in restaurants either owned or patronized largely by foreigners. In the summer of 1990, rock parties were held in places like Maxim's (a French-owned restaurant), the bar at the International Hotel, the Restaurant for Foreign Diplomatic Missions, and the like. There are two reasons for the use of this strategy. First, foreign restaurant owners are more willing to take on the political risk of sponsoring such an event than their Chinese counterparts. Second, the Public Security Bureau (i.e., the police) is much less willing to disrupt an event taking place in such a space, which is unofficially granted a certain measure of extra-territoriality. In the summer of 1990, the single party that was held in a Chinese-owned bar was shut down by the Public Security Bureau several hours before closing time.[43]

The spaces that result from this exclusivity are clearly spaces apart, both literally and metaphorically, from the everyday life of the city. Forms of speech and behavior disallowed in the world outside of the sphere of the

---

[42] Interview with Zhu Xiaomin.

[43] The party took place on June 23, 1990 at the Sunny City Bar (*Taiyang cheng Jiuba*) on Chang'an Avenue near Xidan.

performance become permissible; "bitten tongues created by relations of domination find a vehement, full-throated expression."[44]

This process, of course, resonates with the central aspiration of the rock subculture, the reclamation of an authentic, subjective voice. Moreover, the nature of the performance itself casts the audience in a fundamentally different relation to the performer than that which occurs, for instance, at a televised singing contest. Popularity is not so much a product of participation in the critical activity of the judges, but of communal participation in the communication of authenticity:

> At rock shows, they have the whole audience feeling along with them. They expose all the pain inside of them, and the audiences' hearts beat with them. They yell, and the audience yells. They believe and the audience believes, too.[45]

Gao Qi explains his motivation for performing in a similar way:

> I don't really set out to influence or educate the audience. There's just a feeling...if I can just move the audience with my sincerity, then they'll be right there with me. It's the kind of lifestyle, the *feeling* you get at a rock party... that's what influences people.[46]

Gao Qi's emphasis on "feeling" is telling, for much of the emotional release afforded party-goers is a product of the sheer physicality of listening to loud rock music, yelling, chanting, and dancing. Scott, drawing on the work of the Russian literary theorist M.M. Bakhtin, utilizes the notion of "carnival" to explicate the ritual spaces created by dissident subcultures. In carnival:

> Normal rules of social intercourse are not enforced, and either the wearing of actual disguises or the anonymity conferred by being part of a large crowd amplifies the general air of license...carnival emphasizes the spirit of physical abandon, its celebration of the body through dancing...open sexuality, and general immodesty. Carnival... allows certain things to be said, certain forms of social power to be exercised that are muted outside this ritual sphere...it [is] the only place where

---

[44] Scott, 120.
[45] Interview with Hu Yue.
[46] Interview with Gao Qi.

> undominated discourse prevails, where there is no servility,
> false pretences, obsequiousness...the carnivalesque was a realm
> of release.[47]

The rock party is clearly just such a realm. Party-goers, sporting outlandish hairstyles and clothing, drink, yell, flirt with each other, dance uninhibitedly, and scream along with songs that in any other social context would undoubtedly be denounced as spurring on wholesale "bourgeois liberalization" and "spiritual pollution."

The Tutu Band's performance of their song "There's Only Today" (*Zhi you jintian zai yanqian*) at a rock party held at the Ritan Restaurant in Beijing provides a clearer view of the dynamics of rock music, lyrics, and the 'carnivalesque' atmosphere of rock performances.[48] The Ritan Restaurant, which caters largely to foreign embassy personnel, is inside an elegant Chinese-style building set in a park in the heart of Beijing's diplomatic compound. The party in question was held in a traditional style courtyard--complete with a rockery and goldfish pond—within the restaurant's grounds. A low makeshift stage was erected on one side of the courtyard; on the other was a bar dispensing beer and snacks. Within this highly unusual, circumscribed space were about four hundred musicians, private entrepreneurs, artists, college students, foreign students and embassy workers.[49]

On stage, the Tutu Band—decked out in jeans, t-shirts, and spiky, punk haircuts—lurch into "There's Only Today." Zhu Xiaomin, with an intensity that can only be described as manic, begins the performance with a recitation of a few selected lines of the lyric:

> All the oppression of the past
> I can't bear today!
> All the happiness I have today
> I know won't be enough for the future!

At this point, the audience erupts into a collective affirmation: "Right!"

---

[47] Scott, 173-5. See M.M. Bakhtin, trans. Helene Iswolsky, *Rabelais and His World*, (Bloomington: Indiana University Press, 1984).

[48] Live recording, Ritan Park, Beijing, July 8, 1990.

[49] It should be noted that the foreigners in attendance tended to participate somewhat less actively than Chinese. Generally speaking, the dancers crowding the space immediately in front of the stage were Chinese, while many foreigners (perhaps inured to the sheer novelty of rock music) tended to remain on the peripheries of the courtyard.

I just want to realize all of the portents yesterday made for today
I don't want to make any hypocritical compromises with myself!

The audience responds with an even more passionate, "Good!" The song begins with thirty-two measures in which a slow tempo is coupled with a recurring minor, arpeggiated chord. Over this harmonically static musical structure, Zhu pensively delivers the following verses:

What you and I have already felt is the past
What you and I have imagined is the future
There's only today in front of our eyes

What you and I have gathered up is the past
What you and I will create is the future
There's only today in front of our eyes

Minor harmonies, as Gao Qi comments, are often used by Chinese rock musicians to evoke a sense of oppression (*yayi*) in the listener.[50] If the first thirty-two bars are evocative of the "oppression of the past," then the following eight signal a decisive breakthrough to the release afforded by a ringing rejection of that past. The drums, bass guitar and rhythm guitar break into double-time. The acceleration of the tempo and the pounding homophony of the band provide the audience with a *visceral* sense of excitement and release. The audience begins to leap up and down *en masse*, breaking into a spontaneous, collective chant in time with the staccato rhythms. In the next thirty-two measures, Zhu triumphantly sings out the verses he had recited at the beginning of the performance over a major harmonic progression that repeatedly descends to resolution in a tonic chord. The audience claps in time as it dances, crying out its approval.

The remainder of the song continues to exploit this structure of tension and release, oppression and its negation. The audience becomes increasingly boisterous, bouncing and careening off one another in the closely packed space in front of the stage. One band later, when Cui Jian makes a surprise (and, in the eyes of the Beijing municipal government, illegal) appearance, his performance of the song "Like a Knife" is drowned out by the chaotic chants and roars of the crowd. The "bitten tongue" of Beijing's rock subculture has found a unified, "full-throated voice."

---

[50] Interview with Gao Qi.

Is this collective release an emancipatory event? Or does it merely serve as a kind of negotiated "safety-valve," allowing rock fans to let off steam instead of throwing themselves into forms of political action that could effect a more enduring release from oppression? The answer undoubtedly lies somewhere in between these two poles. The meaning of a given fan's use of the music and its milieu remains mercurial. Outside of the ritual sphere, different party-goers have different levels of commitment to the oppositional ideology which is given voice at the rock party. For some fans, a rock party may just be a chance to let loose, to scream and shout in relative safety and anonymity. For others, including the majority of rock musicians themselves, participation is seen as one manifestation of the individualism and anti-feudalism upon which the whole subculture is founded. Short of undertaking detailed empirical analysis of the expectations and attitudes of each participant, no hard and fast conclusions can be drawn.

There are, however, several strong theoretical arguments that refute an interpretation of the rock party as mere "safety-valve." First, the CCP's policy towards the rock subculture has not been modelled according to the notion that rock "serves to displace and relieve social tensions, and hence restore social harmony."[51] Instead, the CCP has and continues to ban large-scale rock concerts, as well as the release of rock recordings. As I mentioned earlier, even small-scale rock parties have been shut down, or banned altogether (in the case of Cui Jian). In short, the CCP has not so much "removed the stopper to stop the bottle from being smashed altogether" as forced rock music's subversive energies ever deeper into the bottle of subcultural marginalization.[52]

Second, as Scott notes, the "safety-valve theory" is rooted in a psychological fallacy. Temporary emotional release does not inevitably result in long-term political passivity:

> Why is it that a ritual modeling of revolt should necessarily diminish the likelihood of actual revolt? Why couldn't it just as easily serve as a dress rehearsal...?[53]

Finally, I am unsure as to whether such collective expressions of defiance should even be relegated to the role of "dress rehearsal." In the wake of the Tiananmen demonstrations, direct political action is prohibitively

---

[51] Scott, 177.
[52] Roger Sales, as cited in Scott, 177.
[53] Scott, 178.

dangerous. The indirect cultural defiance that occurs at rock parties may be less a safety-valve than a relatively safe way to keep the spirit of 1989 alive. In explaining the significance of the rapid growth of the rock subculture since the crackdown, one rock musician comments:

> We're suffering from oppression. When the oppression comes down too hard, people have to get out from under it. That's why the movement broke out last year. But now, if you want to express your dissatisfaction, you can't go out and demonstrate, or make a speech. You would be arrested right then and there. So, we've had to change our means of expression. That's what rock is all about.[54]

---

[54] Personal interview, Beijing, July 1990. These comments were made 'off the record.'

5

CUI JIAN AND THE IDEOLOGY OF CHINESE ROCK MUSIC

Rock is an ideology, not a set musical form.

—Cui Jian

Rock's engagement in the ideological struggles of 'new era' China has not been restricted to the circumscribed subcultural space of the rock party. In the last chapter, I recounted the ways in which rock music is produced and performed in a oppositional, subcultural milieu. Such a milieu, of course, does not grow in complete isolation. Much of rock's ideological force derives from its interactions with the public sphere. Because of the infiltration of that sphere by China's most popular rock musician, Cui Jian, the genre has exercised a profound—and in the view of the CCP, subversive—influence on a larger youth culture shared by China's college students (and to a lesser extent, private entrepreneurs). The sensibilities of both this youth culture and the rock subculture, in turn, bear the marks of the kind of struggles over the nature of a modernized Chinese cultural identity I discussed in relation to the television documentary *River Elegy* in chapter two. Finally, I argue—through an analysis of two of Cui Jian's songs and the way in which they are used by their audiences—that rock music's presence in the public sphere not only provides a wider audience of rock fans with the kind of affective empowerment and emotional release I described taking place in the subcultural world of the rock party, but also with a vehicle for public expressions of political dissent.

Rock Music and Subculture

In chapter two, I asserted that ideological conflict in *tongsu* music is manifested through the music's participation in the public sphere. This sphere is essentially coterminous with the mass media. The ideological struggles in which *tongsu* music plays an essential role are waged on television, over the airwaves, by audio-cassette, and in print. These struggles are efforts on the part of various groups to provide audiences with authoritative definitions of Chinese culture and society in order to either retain or combat hegemony. Because the CCP actively disapproves of rock's ideological stance, the music has largely been barred from these media. If rock music as well as *tongsu* music is an agent of such struggle, then how and where is that struggle taking place? I propose that rock music operates in the context of an *alternative* public sphere, one whose activities and ideological aims are constituted outside of and in opposition to the mass media (and its hegemonic boundaries). If *tongsu* music is a mass cultural phenomena, then the site of the *production* of ideological contention in rock music might be called *subcultural*.

By 1990, a well-defined rock music subculture had begun to emerge in Beijing.[1] This subculture is similar in many ways to youth subcultures in Western, industrialized nations.[2] Subcultural theory has been a major focus of the work of the Birmingham School of cultural studies I discussed in relation to the notion of "recontextualization." These theorists have broadly defined subcultures as:

> ...meaning systems, modes of expression or lifestyles developed by groups in subordinated structural position in response to dominant meaning systems...which reflect their attempt to solve structural contradictions arising from the wider societal context.[3]

The identity of subcultural groups is usually defined in terms of its members' intensive involvement with a specific musical genre, with the "mode of expression" that best articulates the lifestyle and values of its participants. Group activities are centered around the production,

---

[1] The Chinese term for "subculture," "*ya wenhua*," literally indicates an "oppressed culture." The word has only recently been introduced into the language through translations of Western scholarly work on the issue. The word "*ya wenhua*" is not as yet in general use. When questioned as to whether or not the rock scene could be characterized as a "*ya wenhua*," rock musicians always asked for a definition of the word, and then affirmed that what they referred to as the "rock culture" [*yaogun wenhua*] was indeed a "*ya wenhua*."

[2] Rock music subcultures have also been in existence in the Soviet Union and Eastern European nations like Czechoslovakia and Poland since the late 1970's. While there are clearly instructive comparisons to be drawn between these socialist subcultures and the Chinese rock scene, the paucity of *theoretical* literature on Eastern European subcultures has led me to restrict this discussion to Anglo-American models.

[3] Michael Brake, *Comparative Youth Culture: The Sociology of Youth Culture and Youth Subcultures in America, Britain, and Canada*, (London and New York: Routledge & Kegan Paul, 1985), 8.

consumption, and discussion of music. Members of a subcultural group identify themselves to society and each other through slang, clothing, hairstyles, and behavior that deliberately transgress social norms, and in doing so mount "symbolic challenges to a symbolic order."[4] These challenges often involve ironic recontextualizations of symbols drawn from the dominant culture in acts of what Dick Hebdige terms "semiotic guerrilla warfare."[5]

British observers of subcultural phenomena like Hebdige and Stuart Hall have stressed the importance of the symbolic in their studies of postwar working class subcultures (Mods, Teddy Boys, Punks, Skinheads) in Britain.[6] These groups, in their view, arise in order to confront the socioeconomic problems faced by the youth who create and participate in them. Their solutions to these problems, though, are largely of an expressive and symbolic nature; subcultures provide "a pool of available symbolic resources which particular individuals or groups can draw on in their attempt to make sense of their own specific situation and create a viable identity."[7] The subcultural rebellion usually occurs not in the realm of concrete political activity, but in terms of a revolt against cultural hegemony in music and fashion: their "rebellion seldom reaches [the level of] articulated opposition."[8] This rebellion is invariably met with outrage, stiff resistance, and eventually, co-optation from the dominant culture.

Beijing's rock scene bears many of the marks of an emergent subculture as described by theorists like Hall and Hebdige. In one important respect, however, the Chinese case differs from the Birmingham model. For while the Chinese rock subculture has not reached the level of articulated *political* opposition, the rock sensibility does hinge upon a clearly articulated, self-consciously held ideology of *cultural* opposition. Moreover, this restriction to the realm of culture is less a product of the inherent limitations of the subculture, than the fact that overt political insubordination is not a viable option in post-Tiananmen China. I will return to this notion of cultural opposition later in the chapter, after first detailing some of the more concrete indices of rock music's status as a subcultural form.

---

[4] Dick Hebdige, *Subculture: The Meaning of Style*, (London: Routledge, 1987), 92.

[5] Ibid., 91.

[6] See Stuart Hall and Tony Jefferson, eds., *Resistance Through Rituals: Youth Subcultures in Post-war Britain* (London: Hutchison, 1976).

[7] Brake, 27.

[8] Ibid., 7.

Chinese rock musicians and fans are a close-knit social group comprised of no more than several hundred people. Lacking any affiliation with work units, their activities center around rehearsals and rock parties. Audiences at rock performances are composed of rock musicians and rock fans (a group that includes members of another significant subcultural group, young private entrepreneurs (*getihu*), as well as students and artists). This cohesiveness as a group is also attested to by frequent non-musical communal activities and social gatherings.[9]

Participants are not necessarily linked by any common social or educational class background as is frequently the case in British and American working-class subcultures. Rock musicians include college graduates and professionally trained musicians as well as high school drop-outs and working-class youth.[10] While theorists like Brake have linked participation in subcultural groups to specific age groups (usually those situated between completing their education and joining the work force), no such hard and fast rules can be drawn in the case of Chinese rock and rollers.[11] Ages vary between 16 and 32 years of age. Older and/or more highly educated musicians tend to take the lead in defining the cultural and political agendas underlying rock activities, while asserting that younger musicians are perhaps more representative of a "true" rock sensibility because of their deeper absorption of western culture and greater degree of rebelliousness.[12]

They are all linked, however, by styles of dress, language, and behavior. Rock musicians share a lexicon of musical terms unintelligible to much of the general population. Further, offensive language is pervasive; sentences are littered with "fucks" and "goddamns." For men, long hair, spiky punk hair-styles, torn jeans, t-shirts, studded leather jewelry, and sunglasses—all drawn from the sartorial lexicon of punk rock and heavy metal—are common. The wholesale adoption of Western styles

[9] Nearly every Sunday afternoon in the summer of 1990, for instance, groups of up to forty rock musicians and fans congregated for an afternoon of soccer and swimming.

[10] These observations are by no means intended as a scientific assessment of rock demographics. They are based on the comments of perhaps 30 participants in the rock scene.

[11] Another important characteristic of Western subcultures is male domination. Music, styles and activities all center around males and masculinity. Females tend to be relegated to being mere fans, groupies, or hangers-on. While the majority of Chinese rockers are indeed male, there are several exceptions. Wei Hua, a former anchorwoman for CCTV, is the lead singer of the Breathing Band (*Huxi yuedui*), and one of the most charismatic and well-known figures in Chinese rock. The "Women's Band" (*Nuzi dui*) have also performed frequently in Beijing, and insist on their autonomy from male musicians. For brief profiles of Wei Hua and the Women's Band, see Tong Wei, 18-21.

[12] Interviews with Liu Xiaosong, Beijing, June 23 and 29, 1990.

is itself a highly significant gesture. In a genre that takes as a central goal the repudiation of much that is traditionally "Chinese," "Western" clothes and hair-styles that "epater les Chinoises" are precisely the point. Other, more 'indigenous' fashions are also popular. Cui Jian's insistence on performing in battered PLA khakis and "Mao suits" is a notable example of a subversive sartorial recontextualization.[13] Others, particularly women, wear "exotic" clothing and accessories drawn from the traditional garb of minority peoples within the P.R.C. Style, as Hebdige points out, is one of the central "symbolic resources" upon which subcultures draw in their efforts to undermine cultural hegemony. The specific types of styles adopted by any one subcultural group, in turn, are necessarily expressive of the nature of the group's cultural agenda:

> [Our style] represents our attitude, and also has a psychological value. When you have hair down to your shoulders, everybody looks at you on the street. It naturally draws attention to you. It sounds superficial, but in the Chinese tradition you're supposed to be reserved and discreet, and we need to break through this restriction.[14]

Is the rock subculture, as the Birmingham scholars argue, a response on the part of rock musicians to the pressures brought to bear upon them by "structural contradictions arising from the wider social context"? The most urgent concern expressed by rock musicians, in interviews and in song lyrics, is the need to rebel against oppression (*yayi*). *Yayi* is conceived of as a cultural problem, as the stifling of individual expression and creativity brought about by an authoritarian, conformist, and 'feudal' cultural tradition. Feudalism (*fengjian zhuyi*) is seen to pervade every aspect of social and political life. In a broad (and somewhat speculative) sense, then, the "structural contradiction" encountered by the rock subculture can be seen as resulting from contradictions inherent to the program of economic reform and opening to the West that has been implemented since 1979. Economic reform and material progress have not been matched with commensurate gains in political liberty or individual freedom. This

---

[13] Another example of the inscription of rock ideology in clothing is a t-shirt designed by Cui Jian himself, which depicts two brick walls joined at the top by a string of barbed wire. Between the wall is a green plant in the shape of the Chinese character for "person" (*ren*). The whole picture—of a "person" in a box—forms another character, "jail" (*qiu*).

[14] Interview with Gao Qi.

discontinuity, as many observers have noted, also lay at the root of the student movement of 1989.[15]

This problem is often experienced in terms of generational difference, as was intimated in Liu Suola's "A Superfluous Story" by the Propaganda Chief's disdain for the young workers he claims to represent, and Xiao Hu's final revision of the song she has been commissioned to write:

> What made you lose your youth and at the same time not be able to stand seeing other people's youth?[16]

Youth, here, is seen less as a function of actual age, than as an idealized quality, a sensibility. This sensibility is largely a product of economic reform and liberalization; young people in the past ten years have been exposed to unprecedented doses of Western culture. At the same time, the sheer rapidity of social and cultural change in the 'new era' has resulted in the creation of a widening generation gap. Rock musicians are acutely aware of this generation gap, and cite the formative influence of Western popular culture as a central factor in stirring them towards individualism and rock music. Gao Qi, a twenty-two year old rock musician, explains rock's reaction against *tongsu* music in generational terms:

> *Tongsu* music is written for an older audience. Rock is youth music...young people need to express themselves. They are in the process of developing their opinions, their identities...In China, we have several thousand years of feudalism, which makes people's thinking all alike, conformist, without individualism. Now, after reform and liberalization, you have a generation of youth that are familiar with all sorts of Western things and Western literature...and this has resulted in a complete cultural transformation...the younger you are, the greater the western influence...the changes have been so fast that the generation gap is like leaping over thousands of years. And rock belongs to this younger generation.[17]

Many of the negative qualities associated with 'feudal culture,' of course, are embodied in the institutional structure and practices of the *tongsu* music industry. Authentic individual expression is suppressed; the

---

[15] This point has been thoughtfully treated by Shen Tong, 113-114.

[16] Liu Suola, 116.

[17] Interview with Gao Qi.

individual is stifled by the group (Hu Yue's "pop music circles," An Dong's song and dance troupe, Jing Gangshan's TV officials). Rock musicians, in contrast, consistently stress that the crux of their ideology lies in an embrace of individualism. One structural manifestation of this value is, of course, the fact that rock musicians write and sing their own songs, and are largely free of the economic or creative exploitation that *tongsu* singers say characterizes their working lives. Even so, it should be borne in mind that the rock subculture, as Cui Jian argues, is not entirely free of social hierarchies or 'feudal' thinking.[18] Indeed, according to both Simmel's classic sociological theory of "Group Expansion and the Development of Individuality," and James C. Scott's notion that dissident groups must maintain a certain degree of conformity in order to effectively cohere, the very narrowness of rock's subcultural milieu tends *not* to stimulate the development of individuality.[19]

Restriction to a subcultural milieu also entails marginalization. Where a televised singing contest reaches audiences of hundreds of millions of people across China, rock parties at bars, restaurants, and college cafeterias in Beijing draw several hundred spectators at most. While cassettes of *tongsu* music are sold at nationalized record and book outlets in cities and towns in every province, rock recordings are often produced at home, duplicated, and passed around through a grapevine of rock listeners (including musicians, artists, *getihu*, and college students) in major metropolitan areas.

Rock Music and Youth Culture

This emphasis on rock's status as a subculture, however, is misleading in one important respect. Rock music has reached a far larger (and more influential) audience than its limited 'base of operations' might indicate. Largely because of the huge popularity of Cui Jian among university students, the *consumption* of rock has become an integral part of a more generalized youth culture centered around urban college campuses.[20] By "youth culture," I indicate the sensibilities and leisure patterns

---

[18] Interview with Cui Jian.

[19] Simmel, 270. This point is borne up by the ironic uniformity of rock lyrics which take individuality as their central theme.

[20] I do not mean to suggest that youth culture in China is monolithic. Rock music is an essential component of university life, but the attitudes and activities of young workers are often quite different. For an journalistic account of a working-class youth culture centered around disco dancing in the industrial city Wuhan, see Randy Chiu, "Disike takes the Floor as youth culture takes the stage," *Far Eastern Economic Review*, May 9, 1985, 61-2.

(consumption of music, literature, etc.) of young people that have not distanced themselves from the mainstream in terms of their institutional affiliations (universities, work-units), aspirations, lifestyles, or through external 'markers' of difference such as distinctive styles of clothing and language.

The popularity of rock music outside of its subcultural milieu has been inextricably linked with college students and youth culture. When rock music has been allowed to be featured at large-scale concerts (as with Cui Jian's Asian Games Tour, and the Modern Music Festival), audiences have been composed largely of students and *getihu*. Cui Jian has performed repeatedly at schools like Beijing University, and students often explore the bars and restaurants where rock parties take place. Such excursions became one component of the intellectual ferment of college life in the late 1980's:

> The 1980's were probably the years when the Chinese people enjoyed the most intellectual freedom they had had since the founding of the People's Republic of China in 1949. I became more aware of this when I entered Beida [Beijing University] and discovered that Western influences were everywhere... When my friends and I went out to various bars in the city, we heard new bands experimenting with rock-and-roll, and Chinese pop music was on everyone's radio at school.[21]

Significantly, Cui Jian's popularity has not been forged exclusively by the mass media: "Chinese pop music" may have been on the radio, but rock music was in the bars. Students are familiar with many Cui Jian songs that have never been officially released, either through seeing performances or hearing the bootleg tapes of those performances that are in wide circulation.[22]

This familiarity, in turn, has exercised considerable influence on the development of student activism in the late 1980's. Indeed, the sensibilities and concerns of rock musicians and student activists involved in the Tiananmen democracy movement not only dovetail considerably, but are expressed through an almost identical rhetoric; one that takes as its focus the critique of feudalism in Chinese culture. This is strikingly apparent in a

---

[21] Shen Tong, 113.

[22] From personal observations made during a year spent at Beijing University in 1988-89, I can attest that a strikingly large percentage of students were familiar with Cui Jian's entire repertoire, of which less than half was included on what was at the time his only publicly distributed album, *New Long March Rock*.

speech delivered by one of the most prominent student organizers of the Tiananmen demonstrations, Wu'er Kaixi, on the cultural background of the 1989 movement. His statements serve to illustrate the way in which students both used rock songs like Cui Jian's "I Have Nothing" as a focal point for their own affective investments, and incorporated the insights into their condition gained from the experience of listening to rock into their rhetoric (and in the case of Tiananmen, their political activity):

> Chinese culture is feudalistic, despotic, closed [fengbi]; it negates the individual, and it has lasted for 5,000 years...After 1949 and during the Cultural Revolution this feudalistic culture developed to such an extreme that it now absolutely and completely negates individuality. With reform and the open door policy, and liberalism in thought and culture under Deng Xiaoping, resistance [to feudalism] erupted with full force...In recent years, Chinese college students have been stressing the individual, the self, and rebelling against all sorts of authority...but this idealism and the sense of the individual are contradictory to the reality of present society [so] young people have been left lost and disoriented. The people who are most influential among young people are not [the prominent dissidents] Fang Lizhi and Wei Jingsheng, but...singers such as Cui Jian. His "I Have Nothing"...serves to reflect the sense of loss and the disorientation of Chinese youth.[23]

This set of ideas appears to be nearly identical to those expressed by the keyboard player of the Breathing Band, Dong Dong:

> China is afflicted by feudalism, by conservatism and close-mindedness [fengbi]. The feudal powers [fengjian shili] oppose rock music. Feudal power comes out of blind obedience to Confucian ideals, and relationships between people in society. The open door policy is one way to solve this, but it has been only superficial. People have learned some foreign technologies, but they're still psychologically feudal, and their social circles are still feudal. Even some of the rock musicians' long hair is a sign of this superficial approach to Westernization. We don't want to change the world, but we do want to challenge feudalism with a kind of

---

[23] Wu'er Kaixi, transcript of panel discussion, "Chinese Writers Under Fire: The Struggle for Human Rights in China", in *Pen American Center Newsletter*, #70 (December 1989), 19.

spiritual liberalization [*jingshen shang de kaifang*], to help each individual solve these problems on a psychological level, through individual freedom.[24]

Clearly, there is only a fine line between the rhetoric of Dong Dong's brand of cultural activism and the more explicitly politicized objectives of student activists. The political goals of student activists active in planning the Tiananmen movement echo the cultural critique of rock musicians, and their sense of inter-generational conflict. Shen Tong relates a discussion held by a group of student activists several months before the outbreak of the Tiananmen movement that sheds light on this point:

> China doesn't need a movement for national salvation...what China needs now is personal liberation. What our generation needs to do is push for individual freedom.[25]

While many rock musicians did actively support this agenda through participation in the Tiananmen movement, it is important to remember that their role remained peripheral. Rock musicians do not necessarily share the commitment of student activists to direct political action. Cui Jian claims that rock is a means to make people "*feel* real freedom," not to institute political reform.[26] The distinction is important, even when the realms of cultural and political activism do overlap, as when Cui Jian performed a song, "Opportunists," (*Touji fenzi*) written in praise of the students and their movement, to hunger-strikers on Tiananmen Square:

> Suddenly there was an opportunity
> Everything was empty, we had no goal
> Just like when our mothers gave birth
> And we weren't consulted at all
> What could this opportunity be in the end
> We still haven't thought about it too clearly
> But events have already rushed out of control, seriously
>
> We don't have any experience at all
> And we don't like the past
> But our hearts understand how to keep going
> So there will definitely be some new results

---

[24] Interview with Dong Dong, Beijing, June 21, 1990.

[25] Shen Tong, 150.

[26] Interview with Cui Jian.

We don't know if life requires techniques
Or if we should just get busy and work hard
Anyway, things have already started so we can't be afraid of chaos

Oh, when we get an opportunity we have to express our desire
Oh, when we get an opportunity we have to express our strength...[27]

Interestingly, "Opportunists" is the only song in which Cui Jian strays from his uncompromising individualism by adopting the collective pronoun "we" instead of a singular "I." This suggests that despite the considerable differences in social status and sensibility between the two groups, rock musicians and students, at least in the context of the movement itself, shared a sense of being in it together, if not actual concensus over which "techniques" to use in "expressing their desire."

Rock Ideology and the Public Sphere

Rock music has been perceived by college students and private entrepreneurs as articulating many of their own pressing political and cultural concerns. What accounts for the similarity of the individualist, anti-feudalist rhetoric shared by rock devotees and college students? One important link between the two groups is the mass media. College students and rock musicians have listened to the same *tongsu* music, watched the same films, and read many of the same books, magazines, and newspapers. Each group acknowledges the influence of Western popular music, literature and art on the development of their generation's sensibilities. Finally, both student activists and rock musicians claim to be indebted to the works of "misty" poets like Bei Dao, Gu Cheng, and Yang Lian.[28]

Rock in Print

It is important to bear in mind that for the average college student, rock music remains an extremely novel, even somewhat mysterious, form

---

[27] "Touji fenzi" [Opportunists], music and lyrics by Cui Jian, on *Jiejue*.

[28] The definitive collection of "misty poetry" is Lao Mu, ed. *Xin shichao shiji* [Collected poems of the new wave], (Beijing: Beijing daxue wusi wenxue she Weiming hu congshu bian weihui, 1985. Several of the songs in the repertoire of Zhu Xiaomin's Tutu Band are actually poems by a minor misty poet, Da Ta, set to rock music. See translation of Tutu Band's "Yexu conglai jiushi cuo" [Perhaps it's always been wrong] in the appendix. Similar experiments have been carried out by the avant-garde poet Hei Dachun, whose work appears in Lao Mu, ed., 751-3.

of music. Sources of information regarding rock music (either in its Western or Chinese form) are extremely scarce. Rock music, as I have repeatedly stressed, is barred from television (and for the most part) radio broadcast. Short of actually attending a rock party, a college student interested in rock music would have to turn to the print media (including books, newspapers and magazines, and journals) in order to formulate a notion of just what underlies the rock sensibility. For this reason, the portrayal of rock in the print media has had an important influence on the way in which rock is perceived and used by the larger youth culture.

The print media, of course, is itself a forum for ideological struggle. Rock has been both attacked and praised by the media. I will focus here on the few positive appraisals of the music that appeared in the year before the Tiananmen movement, in order to show that rock as a genre has indeed been linked by its commentators to youth culture and oppositional politics.[29]

Zheng Xiangqun, writing in July of 1988 for the journal *People's Music* on "The Characteristics of Rock Music," characterizes the genre in terms of the ways in which youth in Western nations has used the music as an instrument of social protest:

> To sum up, rock is the expression [*faxie*] of the discontent young people feel towards the status quo...[and] the social system... it is not simply a type of music, but has become a sort of religion for young people, an indispensable means for them to communicate their ideals...and struggle to implement them.[30]

For Zheng, this function means that rock becomes an arena in which "intense ideological conflicts" are stirred into explosive life:

---

[29] It should be noted that Cui Jian's Asian Games tour prompted a barrage of positive articles in several prominent youth-oriented magazines. See Mu Mu, "Tianbian gunlai de gesheng" [The sound rolling down from the sky], *Qingnian yuekan*, 1990/ 5, 17-21. Also see Ma Mu and Ping Fang, "Yiwu suoyou, yaogun yu touji: wei Yayun hui juankuan yibaiwan yuan yiyan jishi" [I have nothing, rock and opportunism: a record of Cui Jian's tour to raise one million yuan for the Asian Games], *Xiju shijie*, 1990/ 3-4, 2-11. In addition, the March 1990 issue of *Daxuesheng* [University students] appeared in April with both front and back covers adorned with color pictures from Cui Jian's Asian Games tour. Strangely enough, the issue did not include an article on the tour, suggesting that the subject had become politically volatile after its sudden cancellation.

[30] Zheng Xiangqun, "Yaobai yue jiqi tezheng" [The characteristics of rock music], *Renmin yinyue*, 1988/7, 43.

...in West Germany, a two-day rock festival against Neo-Nazism took place, and was attended by 30,000 youths from all over the country. The government mobilized 5000 military police, as well as armored vehicles. Helicopters circled overhead to maintain order...[31]

Finally, Zheng claims this volatile genre for the "people," asserting that rock reflects the "struggles of the masses against oppression."[32] Zheng's position, of course, eclipses even the most optimistic accounts of rock music given by leftist critics in the West, as well as surpassing the comparatively modest claims of Chinese rock musicians themselves. More important is the fact that rock seems to be entering public discourse not in terms of musical style, but of its potential as a vehicle for ideological and inter-generational, conflict.

Xiao Feng, in an essay called "Cui Jian: China's John Lennon," provides the Chinese reader with a similar, if somewhat less radical, reading of the nature of rock music in the West. The essay itself appeared in a mass market paperback, *Kings of Contemporary Song* (*Dangdai gewang*), and was intended for a far larger and considerably less scholarly audience than that of a musicological journal like *People's Music*. In addition, *Kings of Contemporary Song* was the only book on popular music available at Beijing University's bookstore in the months preceding the Tiananmen movement, and thus presumably attained a considerable readership among Beijing college students. Xiao, in the process of demystifying for his readers the genre in which Cui works, relates the history of rock music in the West:

Rock music is a form of popular music that arose in the United States in the 1950's and rapidly became a global phenomenon. It is the product of the combination of the popular music of American blacks, the blues, and white country music. To the accompaniment of its varied rhythms, deafening electric guitars, and electric keyboards, the rock singer uses his own thick, hoarse voice to give vent to the troubles and sadness in his heart, as well as criticizing the commonly shared social problems of the millions. Because it dealt with the serious philosophical problems of human life, it was received with excitement, and quickly swept across all of

---

[31] Ibid., 43.
[32] Ibid.

Europe and America. The English rock star John Lennon formed the Beatles with three partners from the working-class city of Liverpool. The Beatles clashed with traditional English culture, and defiantly declared their independence from the sentimental popular music [*tongsu yinyue*] of the time.[33]

This, of course, is a highly selective reading of rock history, one that neglects to include any number of ways rock music has functioned in the Anglo-American context. Rock has not always taken "serious philosophical problems of human life" as its focus. Nor do all rock singers gruffly sing of their frustrations and those of the masses. The Beatles did spring from the working-class rock subculture of Liverpool, but their early music had less to do with a disavowal of "sentimental tongsu music" than a revolution of musical style and image. In short, John Lennon comes to resemble Cui Jian more than Cui Jian resembles John Lennon; the passage reveals more about Chinese reconstructions of the nature and social function of rock than its actual form in the West.

Thus, critical discourse on rock music (as well as the self-assessment of rock musicians) is infused with a remarkable earnestness, with a sense that rock music, by its very nature, is engaged in the articulation of social conflict. Cui Jian's songs, according to one critic, are not simply fun to sing and dance along with; instead they represent a "deadly serious frivolity."[34] Serious consideration of the socio-political implications of popular music, of course, is not a novelty in Chinese critical discourse on popular music; as Jin Zhaojun notes, Chinese music criticism is "inseparable from sociology."[35] What is important about the frequency with which rock is linked by critics to social conflict (particularly conflict across generation lines) is that it has facilitated and in some sense legitimated the appropriation of rock music by student activists as a tool for ideological struggle. For it is only in the presence of such a discourse that a student activist like Wu'er Kaixi can plausibly declare that Cui Jian exercised a far more profound influence on the democracy movement than the two most celebrated democratic dissidents in recent Chinese history, Wei Jingsheng and Fang Lizhi.

---

[33] Xiao Feng, 2-3. Similar Chinese readings of Western rock music can be found in Gu Tu's *People's Daily* article on Cui Jian, as well as Jin Zhaojun's "Cui Jian yu Zhongguo yaogun yue" [Cui Jian and Chinese rock], in *Renmin yinyue*, 1989/4, 32-33.

[34] Ren Zhen, "Cui Jian yu Zhongguo yaogun chao."

[35] Interview with Jin Zhaojun.

Rock Ideology and *River Elegy*

The ideologies and self-perceptions of both student activists and rock musicians are also clearly indebted to the 'cultural self-reflection' of *River Elegy*. On the heels of the film's first broadcast in 1988, entire universities devoted full days to viewing and discussing the film. Dru Gladney has convincingly argued that the film's celebration of student activism, and its implicit demand for a political democracy characterized by dialogue and "transparency," had a formative influence on the way in which the Tiananmen movement unfolded. Students, appropriating many of the images and techniques of student activism shown in *River Elegy*, demanded direct, public dialogue with the senior leaders of the CCP.[36]

The influence of *River Elegy* on the ideological positions of rock musicians is considerably less direct. Fittingly, River Elegy engaged the imaginations of rock musicians not as a political agenda, but as a way in which to understand and discuss the ostensible "feudalism" of Chinese culture, and rock's own anti-feudal stance. Rock musicians often discuss their music in terms of the temporal and geographical axes (from feudal Chinese tradition to western modernity, from the stagnant Northwest to the vibrant southeastern coast and the ocean) around which the writers of River Elegy structured their critique of Chinese culture. When asked "How would you define Chinese rock?" several respondents unhesitatingly prefaced their responses with, "China has a five thousand year tradition of feudalism..."[37] Each interviewee went on to interpret rock music as a manifestation of a conflict between feudalism and modernity. Again, their language echoed that of River Elegy: Feudal culture is "landlocked/ closed" (*fengbi*), while the rock sensibility is "liberalized/open" (*kaifang*). Cui Jian's own assessment of the cultural function and value of rock music, for instance, relies on a metaphor that quite obviously derives from the film:

> Chinese history and Chinese culture are very long and very rich. But right now our culture is like a river without an exit, without a way out to the ocean. The river's moving, but we don't know where it's heading. What we want to do is find a

---

[36] Dru Gladney, lecture on "Tiananmen: Retrospection and Mediation," New England China Seminar, Harvard University, March 20, 1990. *River Elegy* included footage of the epochal May 4, 1919 student movement, as well as shots of the student demonstrations for democracy that swept across many major Chinese cities in the winter of 1986-7. In addition, the film included a short segment on the use of hunger-striking as a political weapon—a method that, before Tiananmen, had never been employed by activists in China.

[37] As in interviews with Cui Jian, Dong Dong, Gao Qi, and Zhu Xiaomin, Beijing, June-July, 1990.

way to release this river, to find an outlet for it, to let it flow
into the ocean, and join with the world outside China. We
want to create a new culture, a culture that isn't parochial and
closed in on itself.[38]

This dichotomy of feudalism and modernity, of an insular China
placed in opposition to the outside world, was also utilized by rock
musicians as a way to criticize *tongsu* music. Zhu Xiaomin believes that:

Rock has become an international phenomenon because it's a
direct expression of basic human desires, of our unlimited
capacities. Human personality is the same everywhere;
everyone needs to express themselves...I don't like Chinese
folk songs, or *tongsu* music that's based on Chinese folk
music. All it can express is a closed [*fengbi*] parochial
nationalism. If you're singing about China, you can't sing
about yourself, about your own basic human desires.[39]

Questioned about the relation between rock, *River Elegy*, and
Westernization, one musician comments:

I still get my inspiration from China itself, not the West. But
I understand and totally agree with the points made by *River
Elegy*. Without that kind of negation [of traditional culture],
there won't be any forward movement... I have the same
thoughts, and I want to express these kinds of views about the
world and society, but obviously I can't do it too directly.
Maybe I've said too much...[40]

This musician's anxiety reflects both the determination of rock
musicians to maintain a low political profile, as well as the extent to which
River Elegy had become an ideological hot potato by the summer of 1990.

Even so, He Yong, a musician whose outrageous stage antics and
uncompromisingly rebellious stance have earned him notoriety as Beijing's
foremost exponent of punk rock, does not shy away from penning lyrics
that make *River Elegy*'s proposals for cultural reform seem mild in
comparison:

[38] Cui Jian, as interviewed in the television documentary *China Rocks: The Long March of
Cui Jian*, (BBC-TV, dir. Greg Lanning, 1991).
[39] Interview with Zhu Xiaomin, July 19, 1990.
[40] This comment was "off the record."

"Garbage Dump" (*Lajichang*)

The place where we live
is like a garbage dump
The people are like insects
Everyone's struggling and stealing
We eat our consciences and it's ideology that we're shitting

Sure, there's a green tree growing
You can smell the flower's scent
The Forbidden City's really pretty
There's even a really great wall
They're growing on top of a garbage dump

The place where we live
is a slaughterhouse
All you have to know is dirt
And you're already good enough to be sold in pounds and ounces
Cixi's foot-binding cloth was long and stinky

Is this a joke?
No!
Tear it down!
Is this a joke?
No!
Tear it down![41]

Where *River Elegy* proposed the deconstruction of outdated, even perniciously backward, symbols of the insularity of Chinese culture like the Great Wall, He Yong cries for their immediate demolition. The Great Wall and the Forbidden City have come not just to symbolize the insularity of a culture that has died young and must be revitalized along Western lines, but a culture that eats its own.[42] The song—performed with heavily distorted electric guitar, erratic changes of tempo, and screamed vocals that verge on

---

[41] "Lajichang" [Garbage dump], music and lyrics by He Yong. Live recording, Ritan Park, Beijing, July 7, 1990. An earlier version of the song ended by demanding "Is there hope?/If not/Tear it down." Until 1989, He Yong was the lead singer for Mayday [*Wuyue tian*]. He has since become an independent singer/songwriter. For an interesting portrait of He Yong and his circle before and after Tiananmen, see the Dutch TV documentary *Out of the Shadows* [*Uit de Schaduw*, Ikon Productions, 1989/91].

[42] This insight is not at all new: Lu Xun's classic short story, "Diary of a Madman" [*Kuangren riji*, 1918] is an allegorical treatment of the 'cannibalism' of traditional culture.

unintelligibility—comes closer than any other Chinese rock song to calling for open revolt against what Dong Dong calls the "feudal power of society." At the same time, the setting of the lyric—"the place where we live"—suggests that "Garbage Dump" is something more than cultural allegory, that tearing down the "feudal power of society" may well be equivalent to fighting the powers that be in contemporary China.

The majority of rock musicians, however, shy away from the kind of overt rebellion exemplified by He Yong's "Garbage Dump." Cui Jian vehemently denies that his work contains any overt political content, and dismisses political uses of his music by audiences as "their own business."[43] Instead, interviewees like Cui Jian, Dong Dong, and Zhu Xiaomin consistently assert that fighting feudalism meant changing people's minds, not their political situation. Cultural change, according to interviewees, must be brought about through personal liberation.

This agenda, of course, is itself quite radical. Dong Dong, in the process of emphasizing the "spiritual liberalization" of the individual as the means through which rock could effect socio-political change, overturned one of the basic tenets of China's ideological hegemony, dialectical materialism:

> It's the way people think and their culture that determines the means of production, not the other way around. And that's how rock might be able to change the way things are.[44]

Cui Jian, whether for fear of being forced into the dangerous role of political dissident or becoming the object of a "cult of personality" among his fans, challenges the idea that his songs represent anything but his own feelings. The implications of his emphasis on subjectivity, however, remain subversive in the Chinese context. On a basic level, expressing the self—without reference to class struggle or the collective—is itself a violation of the CCP's cultural policies and the hegemonic ideology that supports them. This point is illustrated by one of the Propaganda Chief's consultations with Xiao Hu in "A Superfluous Story":

> "'Kissing,' 'losing sleep'—these don't describe the contemporary youth...Then there's the end of the song. It should be 'the people,' not 'ourselves.'"

---

[43] Interview with Cui Jian.
[44] Interview with Dong Dong.

"Aren't we the people? Aren't the people us?"

"No, the people are the people, the people are the *People*. They're not me, and not you, they're not anyone, they're the people."

"Then who would that be?"

"The people."[45]

In re-inserting individuals into a hegemonic discourse concerned with the "People" solely as an abstract political entity, rock musicians attempt to reclaim the power to define themselves and their music.

A further tenet of the rock sensibility is that self-definition —finding one's measuring stick, to borrow Liu Suola's term—will necessarily inspire revolt against feudalism, against the hypocrisy of all those who would be Propaganda Chiefs. What would happen, rock musicians ask, if everyone found their own measuring stick, if authenticity and individualism brought about a larger cultural transformation that rendered feudalism obsolete? Might not such a development inexorably clear the way for positive *political* change? In justifying his claim that his songs are not intended as overt political protest against the CCP, Cui Jian flies in the face of one of the dominant discursive paradigms of the post-1949 period: that culture is subordinate to political concerns:

> [Political protest] doesn't have to be too clear [in my songs]. Governments can temporarily suppress culture, but in reality politics are only just another manifestation of culture.[46]

Cui Jian: "I Have Nothing" but "A Piece of Red Cloth"

Rock songs and rock performances, though, do not necessarily effect the ideological aims of their creators. As I have already pointed out, meaning in popular music is mercurial. Once the music comes into contact with its audience, the ensuing reaction is largely out of the hands of the musician. As a result, rock songs have been used by fans both as a means for affective empowerment, *and* as a conduit for explicitly political protest— whether a musician like Cui Jian claims to like it or not. In order to examine these varying uses of rock music by the larger public that lies outside the confines rock subculture, I will now examine the music, lyrics,

---

[45] Liu Suola, 113.
[46] Interview with Dong Dong.

and reception by audiences of two of Cui Jian's most popular songs, "I Have Nothing" (*Yiwu suoyou*) and "A Piece of Red Cloth" (*Yi kuai hongbu*).

"I Have Nothing" is undoubtedly the most popular song to have emerged from the rock subculture into the public sphere; for many it is virtually synonymous with the term "Chinese rock music." Since 1986, the song has been extensively recorded by a number of *tongsu* singers, exhaustively discussed by Chinese scholars of popular music, and at one point, lavishly praised in an article that appeared in *People's Daily:*

> Why has Cui Jian received such a warm reaction? In order to understand this, we need to go back and listen again to "I Have Nothing." When you hear that melancholy, heavy-hearted tune, when you sing along with those disconsolate lyrics, it always feels like you're spilling out the sadness in your guts...What the song exposes is the feelings of a whole generation: their sadness, their perplexity, the feelings that pour out from the bottom of their hearts. The song's use of the deep, desolate tone of the folk music of the Northwestern plateau, and its coarse rhythms are well suited to this purpose..."I Have Nothing" can also be called the seminal work of Chinese rock. It fuses European and American rock with traditional Chinese music, creating a rock music with a strong Chinese flavor.[47]

The song's lyrics are as follows:

> I've asked tirelessly, when will you go with me?
> But you just always laugh at my having nothing
> I've given you my dreams, given you my freedom
> But you always just laugh at my having nothing
> Oh! When will you go with me?
> Oh! When will you go with me?
>
> The earth under my feet is on the move,
> The water by my side is flowing on,
> But you always just laugh at my having nothing
> Why haven't you laughed your fill?
> Why will I always search?

---

[47] Gu Tu, 5. Several reviews of Cui Jian's work mention the fact that "I Have Nothing" was the talk of a national symposium on popular music held in 1986.

Could it be that before you I will always have nothing?

Oh! When will you go with me?
Oh! When will you go with me?

(*suona solo*)

The earth under my feet is on the move
The water by my side is flowing on

I'm telling you I've waited a long time
I'm telling you my very last demand
I need to grab both your hands
Only then will you go with me
That's when your hands will tremble
That's when your tears will flow
Can it be that you're telling me you love my having nothing?

Oh, only then will you go with me
Oh, only then will you go with me

(*guitar solo*)

The earth under my feet is on the move
The water by my side is flowing on

Oh, only then will you go with me
Oh, only then will you go with me[48]

Stylistically, the song is characterized by its rapidly changing dynamics, its use of instrumental texture to underscore the emotions of the lyric, and the expressive capacities of Cui Jian's rough vocals. Each of these elements reinforces a pattern of stasis and movement, tension and release that is reflected in the lyrics. The song "fades-in" with a sustained chord held for four measures, followed by a verse (16 measures) and a chorus (8 measures) at a slow tempo.[49] At this point, the drums begin to supply a heavy rock backbeat, and the verse/chorus structure is repeated with added

---

[48] Cui Jian, *Xin changzheng lushang de yaogun*.

[49] This song form is typical of Chinese rock music, and is a direct borrowing from Anglo-American popular song form.

intensity. Suddenly, two new instrumental timbres are added. A heavily distorted electric guitar churns out a static minor chord for sixteen measures, over which the *suona* solos. Cui repeatedly sings the lines, "The earth under my feet is on the move/ The water by my side is flowing on," conveying a frustrating sense of immobility. The next section brings release and dynamic motion; just as the tempo doubles and the cymbals and guitars begin to use propulsively syncopated rhythms, Cui forcefully issues his "last demand." Following the chorus, the song reverts to the static minor chord for an impassioned electric guitar solo. Following the final verse, the chorus repeats four times, and the song accelerates to a finish over ever more propulsive bass, guitar, and *suona* lines.

This musical structure of tension and release, of course, is a direct analogue of the affective aims of rock music—a release (*xuanxie*) from oppression (*yayi*) through the assertion of the value of the individual. "I Have Nothing," as with rock music in general, primarily works for its fans "on the affective level of [their] everyday lives, at the level of the strategies [they] use to gain some control over that affective life, to find new forms of pleasure and excitement, or to cope with new forms of pain, frustration, and boredom."[50] That Chinese listeners found "I Have Nothing" affectively empowering in this sense is testified to by a number of accounts. One fan at Cui Jian's Asian Games tour concert in Xi'an expressed the song's power this way:

> When you sing it over and over again, you will learn how to be confident despite hard times, how to awaken yourself from stagnation. You will realize your self-worth after having followed a difficult road.[51]

Another relates that:

> When we sing this song, we don't feel ashamed of having nothing anymore.[52]

A final instance in which "I Have Nothing" served as a means of emotional catharsis is related by the journalists Ping Fang and Ma Mu:

---

[50] Lawrence Grossberg, "Rock and Roll in Search of an Audience," in James Lull, ed., *Popular Music and Communication*, (Newbury Park: Sage Publications, 1987), 186.

[51] Ma Mu and Ping Fang, 6.

[52] Ibid., 6. These comments reiterate almost verbatim those of Gu Tu in a *People's Daily* article of July 16, 1988. Whether Ma Mu and Ping Fang have simply plagiarized that article, or fans have internalized the critical discourse on Cui Jian is unclear.

...the director of a song and dance troupe in Xi'an choreographed "I Have Nothing" for a modern dance. We were invited to the rehearsal. It was a duet...as soon as the music started the two dancers entered deeply into their roles. Before the song had finished, the woman's face was streaming with tears, and the man ran out of the rehearsal space as fast he could. When he came back, his eyes were red, and he said in an unnatural tone, "That song is just too damn moving."[53]

I proposed in chapter two that popular music is one of the only realms in which issues of national concern are expressed through a rhetoric of individual emotion, of affect. I suggest here that this dynamic also informs the intensity of listeners' reactions to "I Have Nothing." Audiences' uses of "I Have Nothing" must be read not only as emotional catharsis, but also in terms of political empowerment, as an allegorical jab at the dominance of the CCP. Interpretations of the lyrics, of course, inevitably vary from listener to listener. A Beijing city official may see the song as a mystifying and subversive denial of the benefits conferred upon China's youth by socialism. Others might hear the story of a love affair between a poverty-stricken young man and a snobbish, rich woman.

Despite this ambiguity, or perhaps because of it, many listeners and critics read the text in terms of political allegory. Tim Brace has suggested that readers of the song lyrics try a simple test: for every "I" substitute a "we," and for every "you," think of the Communist Party.[54] Read in this light, the song becomes an ironic response to the Chinese lyrics of the "Internationale" (*Guoji ge*), a socialist anthem whose ubiquity in Chinese everyday life is second only to that of the national anthem:

> Slaves rise up, rise up!
> We cannot say that we have nothing [*yiwu suoyou*]
> We will be masters of all under heaven[55]

As I have suggested earlier, the substitution of "we" for "I" makes implicit sense both in terms of the politicization that has surrounded Chinese popular music since its inception, and the way in which we enjoy

---

[53] Ma Mu and Ping Fang, 3.

[54] Tim Brace, "Popular Music in Contemporary Beijing: Modernism and Cultural Identity," *Asian Music*, 2 (Spring/Summer 1991), 63.

[55] "Guoji ge," as performed by the China Broadcast Arts Troupe Symphony Orchestra, on *Zhonghua renmin gongheguo guoge, guoji ge* [The national anthem of the People's Republic of China and the Internationale], Zhongguo changpian gongsi HL-314, 1984.

pop music. Much of the pleasure of listening to popular music results from a process of affective investment, from identifying our own passions with those of the singer. This identification, of course, links us not only with the performer, but with the other members of the audience, with a community of shared feeling. The singer's "I" becomes *our* "I." Our "I's," in turn, merge with a collective "we." Cui Jian denies that the song addresses the government, that "I Have Nothing" is equivalent to 'we have no freedom and democracy.' On the streets of Beijing and Hong Kong, however, the use of the song as a marching chant in the spring of 1989 demonstrated that authorial intent may well be besides the point.

"A Piece of Red Cloth"—which unlike "I Have Nothing" has never been officially released in China—is one of the most well-known of Cui Jian's songs among college students and rock fans. "A Piece of Red Cloth" is also perhaps Cui Jian's most complex and disturbing lyric. On March 12, 1989, Cui Jian sang "A Piece of Red Cloth" at the Beijing Exhibition Hall to an audience of 18,000 fans. He fished a bright red cloth from out of the pocket of his PLA jacket, blindfolded himself, and made these prefatory remarks:

> Does everybody still remember the last time I sang this at Beijing Workers Auditorium? Right, it's "A Piece of Red Cloth"... a lot of newspaper reporters who saw that show thought the song was a kind of marriage preview... This feeling really made me comfortable.[56]

He paused, strummed out the first chords of the song, and sang the following lyrics:

> That day you used a piece of red cloth
> to blindfold my eyes and cover up the sky
> You asked me what I had seen
> I said I saw happiness
>
> This feeling really made me comfortable
> made me forget I had no place to live
> You asked where I wanted to go
> I said I want to walk your road
>
> (*saxophone solo*)

---

[56] Live recording, Beijing Exhibition Hall, March 12, 1989.

I couldn't see you, and I couldn't see the road
You grabbed my hands and wouldn't let go
You asked what was I thinking
I said I want to let you be my master

I have a feeling that you aren't made of iron
but you seem to be as forceful as iron
I felt that you had blood on your body
because your hands were so warm

This feeling made me comfortable
made me forget I had no place to live
You asked me where I wanted to go
I said I want to walk your road

(*saxophone solo*)

I had a feeling this wasn't a wilderness
though I couldn't see it was already dry and cracked
I felt that I wanted to drink some water
but you used a kiss to block off my mouth

I had a feeling this wasn't a wilderness
though I couldn't see it was already dry and cracked
I felt that I wanted to drink some water
but you used a kiss to block off my mouth

I don't want to leave and I don't want to cry
Because my body is already withered and dry
I want to always accompany you this way
Because I know your suffering best

Du la, du du du la la, du la... (*saxophone solo*)

That day you used a piece of red cloth
blindfolded my eyes and covered up the sky
You asked me what I could see

I said I could see happiness[57]

In "A Piece of Red Cloth," the 'poetics of authenticity' have become confessional; Cui Jian admits not only the pain of oppression, but his own complicity in the process of subjugation. He is happiest in the blinding, "withering" embrace of his "master." The blood on the hands of his captor is comfortingly warm. Further, the relation of oppressed and oppressed hinges on mutual interdependence; Cui and his captor are locked in a destructive relationship that can only be described as sado-masochistic:

> I don't want to leave and I don't want to cry
> Because my body is already withered and dry
> I want to always accompany you this way
> Because I know your suffering best

In contrast to the rock lyrics I reviewed in the preceding chapter, "A Piece of Red Cloth" presents us with a world characterized by its emotional closure. Rather than rattling the bars of the prison of "suffering" shared by master and subordinate alike, Cui vows to retreat deeper into the cell.

In order to understand the song in terms of the agenda of cultural critique espoused by Cui Jian and his colleagues in the rock subculture, we are compelled to ask who is the "master"? What does the red cloth signify? The color red is a traditional Chinese symbol of matrimony and happiness. At the same time, red cloth inevitably calls to the mind of the Chinese listener the Communist Party and its accouterments: the red flag, the red sun (i.e., Mao Zedong), the ubiquitous red armbands worn by the Red Guards during the Cultural Revolution. The ambiguity of the symbolism of the red cloth, of course, is essential to the song's rhetorical effect. As Scott argues, the expression of subversive critiques of cultural hegemony often hinge upon ambiguity and disguise:

> ...what permits subordinate groups to undercut the authorized cultural norms is the fact that cultural expression by virtue of its polyvalent symbolism and metaphor lends itself to disguise...the condition of [a public expression of dissent] is that it is capable of two readings, one of which is innocuous...[providing] an avenue of retreat when challenged.[58]

---

[57] Cui Jian, music and lyrics.
[58] Scott, 158.

In this sense, the red cloth not only serves to disguise the "master," but the intentions of the "captive" singer as well. The "innocuous" reading of the song, of course, is the one adopted by the newspaper reporters Cui Jian mentions in his prefatory comments—that the song is about the emotional entrapment of marriage. If, however, "A Piece of Red Cloth" is political allegory—and given Cui's disingenuous prefatory comments it is difficult to imagine any other reading—it is less a direct critique of the CCP than an exploration of the problematics of Cui's own submission to power. In the song "Like a Knife" (*Xiang yiba daozi*), Cui proclaims his desire to cut away at his adversary's face until he "sees some truth." Here, the knife is turned in upon himself, and by extension, his audience.

The song's musical structure lacks of the kind of visceral, affective release offered by a song like "I Have Nothing." Cui slowly introduces the melody on his acoustic guitar, playing in halting, almost jagged rhythms. At the same time, the slow, steady chordal support of the electric keyboards establishes a conflicting sense of meditative lyricism. Following the second saxophone solo, the bass guitar and drums kick in, the tempo quickens, and the tension set up by the interplay of guitar and keyboards is temporarily dispelled. At this point, Cui's vocal tone becomes increasingly hoarse, and the rhythm of his delivery of the lyrics more and more irregular. With the lines:

> I don't want to leave and I don't want to cry
> Because my body is already withered and dry
> I want to always accompany you this way
> Because I know your suffering best

Cui's voice becomes constricted to the point that he is producing a kind of quavering rasp. His unpredictable rhythmic accents on the various syllables of each line effectively convey a sense of both vehemence and emotional conflict; the unexpected fury with which he sings the word "accompany" (*peiban*) simultaneously evokes resistance, capitulation, and self-hate. This climactic moment is followed by a series of shouted vocal improvisations ("du du du la la"), matched by the constricted, "screaming" sound of Liu Yuan's saxophone improvisations.

Cui's use of such a broken, highly constricted vocal tone stands in marked contrast with both his own early efforts at rock singing, and with the prevalent singing styles of *tongsu* music.[59] This technique cannot help but emphasize the singer's physicality, to stress the grain of the voice over the immediate intelligibility of the lyrics. This vocal strategy, as John Shephard suggests in a discussion of its use in Anglo-American rock music and the blues, tends to "reproduce physiologically the tension and experiential repression encountered as males engage with the public world."[60] This tension, coupled with the rhythmic discontinuity of his delivery, create a deliberate garbling of the lyrics, as if to suggest that Cui is not only blindfolded, but gagged.

Ultimately, the conflicts and "experiential repression" against which Cui struggles remain unresolved by the performance. The song concludes with a repetition of the first verse. The rhythm section and Cui's tense guitar playing fall away, leaving only the drawn-out chordal underpinning of the keyboards. Cui's vocal tone clears, as does that of Liu Yuan's saxophone; some kind of resolution of the tensions that fueled the performance has been attained. Cui, still blindfolded, his arms hanging limp at his sides, sings:

> That day you used a piece of red cloth
> blindfolded my eyes and covered up the sky
> You asked me what I could see
> I said I could see happiness

Tranquillity has been won at the price of Cui's freedom; "happiness" is found only in submission.

The thinly veiled symbolism of such a performance is not lost on Cui's audiences. Although Cui Jian clearly does not intend "A Piece of Red Cloth" simply as a wholesale condemnation of the CCP, the task of determining the song's meaning does not fall to him alone. While the song lyrics evince a complex understanding of complicity and domination, performances of the song have provided audiences with an occasion for spontaneous, collective demonstrations of political protest. As Cui's contradictory message is appropriated by the audience, its ambiguous, self-reflective contours are flattened. The audience gives "full-throated voice" to

---

[59] Zhang Yimou's "Sister, Go Bravely Forward" is one exception to this rule, but it lacks the rhythm discontinuity and near unintelligibility of Cui's performance.

[60] John Shephard, "Music and Male Hegemony", in Leppert and McClary, eds., *Music and Society: The Politics of Composition, Performance, and Reception*, (Cambridge: Cambridge University Press, 1987), 166.

what Cui himself chose to garble. The red cloth becomes transparent, and Cui's "knife" is once again turned against the "master."

The following description of the inaugural concert of Cui Jian's Asian Games Tour in Beijing is representative of this process, and does much to explicate what led CCP officials to end the tour in mid-career and prohibit Cui from making any further incursions into the public sphere. Of course, much of the poignance of this particular performance lay in the fact that it took place only months after the crackdown at Tiananmen Square:

> In order to raise money for the 11th Asian Games, even this guy has been allowed to give a performance. Nowadays his songs are full of a kind of decadent mood, and he has been prevented from giving many concerts. But yesterday he challenged the authorities again. He sang a forbidden song when the audience encouraged him with passionate applause. He tied a red cloth over his eyes, and his guitarist gagged himself with a red cloth as well. What did this mean? Of course, everyone in Beijing knew exactly what it meant! Most of the audience of 15,000 people rose to their feet. It was so exciting, just like that *other* unbelievable day and night...[61]

---

[61] Personal communication, March, 1990. "That *other* day and night," of course, refers to June 3-4, 1989. These comments were made 'off the record.'

CONCLUSION

"WE DEDICATE THIS KNIFE TO YOU"

In introducing this book, I proposed that Chinese popular music is an arena in which many different voices contend for the "power to construct authoritative definitions of social situations and legitimate interpretations of social needs."[1] The bulk of the study attempts to situate those voices in the context of the generic division between *tongsu* and rock music, and in doing so, characterize how and what these two disparate voices have been 'saying' about what kind of modernity China is advancing towards in the 1980's and 1990's.

In chapter two, I showed that the *tongsu* genre is itself a discursive space within which many voices vie for dominance. The loosening of ideological constraints brought about by economic reform in the 'new era' has allowed for a measure of ideological 'polyphony.' The CCP, of course, has and will continue to engineer popular songs to their own ideological specifications, to offer audiences hegemonic visions of the happiness and abundance that will accompany the attainment of a socialist modernity. Placed on the open market, however, these visions do not always sell; the CCP may attempt to "serve the people," but often the "people" are not buying.[2] Other *tongsu* styles—characterized by 'negotiated' visions of the worrisome cultural predicaments of rapid modernization—have become enormously popular. The "Northwest Wind" gave musical voice to the heated debates on "roots-seeking," feudalism, and modernity that filled China's public sphere in the late 1980's. The potential for 'negotiated' *uses* of *tongsu* music have also been enabled by the state's efforts to "serve the

---

[1] Fraser, *Unruly Practices,* 6.

[2] The Taiwanese rock singer Luo Dayou, in a satirical song about the crackdown on the democracy movement, "Zhuru zhi ge" [The song of the dwarf], presents an ironic metaphor for this process: "In the stock market of struggle the index is enchanting/ the price of revolutionary doctrine is wavering." Music and lyrics by Luo Dayou, on *Airen tongzhi* [Comrade lover], BMG Pacific RC-1001, 1990.

145

people's money," as attested to by the adoption of "jail songs" by disenfranchised private entrepreneurs.

The efforts on the part of songwriters to guide their audiences towards an understanding of "ideological trends"—exemplified by the interaction of *tongsu* music and the television documentary *River Elegy*— have remained within the bounds of 'acceptable' public discourse because of the constraints imposed by the hierarchical institutional structures through which *tongsu* music is produced, performed, and disseminated. Participation in the public sphere necessarily entails tight state supervision. Just as the voices of *tongsu* singers are appropriated by songwriters, work units, and televised singing contests, the voices of songwriters may be pressed to the service of the 'propaganda chiefs' when boundaries recede, as after the crackdown on the Tiananmen movement.

As I discussed in chapter four, the central aspiration of rock musicians is to reclaim an authentic voice that will cut through the "all-englobing web" of hypocrisy that is seen to characterize the world of *tongsu* music, propaganda chiefs, and what Xiao Hu, in "A Superfluous Story" terms "normal ideology." This project has been facilitated by the creation of subcultural spaces outside of the institutional hierarchies of *tongsu* music, spaces where rock musicians and fans are free to develop a 'poetics of authenticity,' to enact collective rituals of release and resistance.

This resistance, however, is not framed in overtly political terms. Instead, rock musicians aim to liberate themselves and their audiences from the depredations of a 'feudal' culture founded on the oppression of the individual. This critique is essentially a radicalization of the cultural anxiety that has pervaded the public sphere in the late 1980's. The authors of *River Elegy* argue that China as a nation must embrace Western conceptions of modernity (i.e., "democracy and science") in order to be revitalized; rock musicians believe that individual Chinese must repudiate what the critic Fan Weiqiang calls "the prescriptive power of traditional culture."[3]

In chapter five, I argued that this subcultural form has been appropriated by a larger youth culture as a vehicle for both affective empowerment and political protest. Rock music has entered public discourse in terms of its capacity as a vehicle for social and inter-generational conflict, as a music that speaks for the "struggles of the masses

---

[3] Su Xiaokang's calls for "democracy and science," of course, self-consciously invoke the memory of the May 4th Movement of 1919. See Fan Weiqiang, 29.

against oppression."[4] This association, coupled with the similarity of rock musicians' anti-feudalist rhetoric to that of student activists, resulted in a situation where students put rock music to direct, politically emancipatory use in the streets and (as with Cui Jian's Asian Games tour) concert halls of Beijing.

If popular music is "like a knife," then it has been wielded by many different groups to cut at a host of disparate cultural and political adversaries. I want to conclude by suggesting that the "knife" cuts deepest when it has claimed for itself the mantle of legitimately speaking for "the people." As Rey Chow notes in a discussion of Chinese popular music:

> The question "Who speaks?" underlies the most brutal of political exterminations. The "who" that is identified through arrests, purges, and murders as the landlords, capitalists, and running dogs is replaced by the "who" that is "the people." Entwined with nationalism and patriotism, and strategically deployed by the state, "the people's speech" that supposedly results from successful class struggle forms the cadences of a sonorous music.[5]

This is precisely the danger Liu Suola identifies in satirizing the efforts of the Propaganda Chief to engineer songs that represent a "people" defined only as "not me, and not you... not anyone, just the *People*."[6] This strategy, as I have shown, is central to the way in which *tongsu* music acts as an instrument for the retention of power. The power to speak for the "people," is ultimately what allows the CCP to construct authoritative visions of Chinese modernity.

As I argued in the introduction, popular music is a double-edged sword; the knife cuts both ways. Rock musicians are not immune from the impulse to speak for the people, to fight for authenticity and cultural transformation *on their behalf*. As the rock subculture is forced ever deeper into the margins of Chinese popular music, the sensibilities of *tongsu* and rock become increasingly polarized. The implicit danger of this development is that the rock subculture may be compelled to define itself

---

[4] Zheng Xiangqun, 43.

[5] Rey Chow, "Listening Otherwise, Music Miniaturized: A Different Type of Question About Revolution," *Discourse* 13 (1), 133-4.

[6] Liu Suola, 113.

and its participants ever more narrowly, to sharpen its ideological blade to a fine point in order to ward off, or even attempt to replace, its adversaries.[7]

Cui Jian himself has consistently disavowed the notion that he "speaks for the people." Even so, his strenuous avoidance of being cast as a spokesman for the rebellious aspirations of young Chinese people cannot obscure the fact that this is precisely what he has become.[8] As one fan comments on his *New Long March Rock* album:

> Cui Jian says things we all feel, but cannot say. We all hate the government. Cui Jian speaks for us. He says my feelings. This is one tape I will keep forever.[9]

Cui Jian's 'message,' as I showed in my discussion of "A Piece of Red Cloth," is far more ambiguous than a simple condemnation of the CCP. He may attempt to deny that he speaks for the people, but once his music enters the public sphere, the people are free to 'speak' for him, to use the knife for their own purposes, whether it is dedicated to them or not:

> "Like a Knife" (*Xiang yi ba daozi*)
>
> My red red heart is gleaming
> Shining on these hands till they look black
> The guitar in my hands is like a knife
> I want to cut your face till all that's left is your mouth
>
> I don't care who you are, my dear
> I want to trade you my blood for your tears
> I don't care if you're an old man or a girl
> I want to cut at your hypocrisy till I get some truth
>
> Zha, zha, zha...
>
> The bare knife is gleaming
> Shining to expose that old man's regrets
> He wrinkles his brows, pouts his lips
> I don't know if it's out of anger or being hurt

---

[7] In this regard, Zhu Xiaomin's comments are instructive. He repeatedly stressed that the "universal truths" embodied by the rock sensibility "will be accepted by the masses," that rock would inevitably come to supplant *tongsu* as the dominant genre of Chinese popular music. Interview with Zhu Xiaomin.

[8] Interview with Cui Jian.

[9] As cited by Brace, 61.

Don't worry, my dear
We weren't born to be enemies
But my rights are like a knife
That wants to lodge itself in this piece of earth

Zha, zha, zha...

Your naked body is gleaming
Shining so that three generations of ancestors are ashamed
You opened your heart
And stretched out your hand
You said what you want is just my sharp blade

You're crying, my dear
I don't know if it's a weak beauty or strong
Now my heart is like a knife
That wants to go through your mouth and kiss your lungs
Zha, zha, zha...[10]

---

[10] Cui Jian, music and lyrics.

APPENDIX

SELECTED *TONGSU* AND ROCK SONG LYRICS

Tongsu lyrics:

The following is a typical tongsu song in what might be called the "revolutionary disco" style taken from the cassette collection *The Whirlwind of '89* (*Guaxiang '89 de da xuanfeng*):

"The Great Undertaking" (*Chuangye*)
music and lyrics: anonymous

The stars shine in the blue sky
The plain is a red bonfire
The hearts of us oil workers face the Party
With deep emotion we're thinking of Beijing

We want to make that plain like a spring, gushing oil
Bravely working, no fear of shedding blood and sweat
In our hearts thinking of Chairman Mao
When the work is bitter and tiring, it's all the sweeter

When the air is chill and the ground frozen
We're not afraid of the cold
Warm blood can thaw the freeze
We oil workers are heroic men

Our happiness is fighting evil winds at the world's edge
Boring into the earth with that big drill
With our own hands we'll break through the rock
Chairman Mao leads us forward
The revolutionary future is so bright

Below are the lyrics for two of the most popular songs to emerge from the Northwest Wind (xibei feng) style that dominated tongsu music in 1988. Both songs are performed by Tian Zhen on a collection of Northwest Wind songs entitled *Shanbei 1988*.

"My Beloved Hometown" (*Wo relian de guxiang*)
music: Xu Peidong
lyrics: Guang Zheng

My hometown isn't pretty at all,
Low thatched cottages, bitter well water
A small stream that usually runs dry
but is reluctant to leave our little village

On a stretch of exhausted earth
we harvest meagre hopes
Dwelled here year after year,
Lived here generation upon generation

Oh! The earth of my hometown that I can't kiss enough,
Water of my hometown that I can't love enough,
I need to use true feeling and sweat
to turn you into fertile earth and lovely water,
fertile earth and lovely water...

Yellow earth always demands more work
There's too little bitter well-water to drink
The men tired of bending their backs plowing for you
The women furrowing their brows for you

Thatched cottages that can't leave
Bitter well water that's supported us
Dwelled here year after year,
Lived here generation upon generation

Oh! Hometown!
Can't kiss the earth of my hometown enough,
Can't love the my hometown's water enough
I need to use my sincerity and sweat
to turn you into fertile earth and lovely water,

fertile earth and lovely water

"Hills of Yellow Earth" (*Huangtu gaopo*)
music: Su Yue
lyrics: Chen Zhe

My home is on high hills of yellow earth
Strong wind blows down from the slopes
It doesn't matter if it's the northwest wind,
Or the southeast wind:
It's all my song, my song.

(repeat)

Doesn't matter how many years and months in the past
Generations of ancestors handed it down to me
Left me a boundless song to sing,
With this Yellow River still by my side

My home is on the high hills of yellow earth
The sun rises up over the slope,
shining into my cave house,
tanning my arms,
then there's my cow and me

My home is on the hills of yellow earth,
All four seasons the wind blows down from the slopes
It doesn't matter if its 800 years,
doesn't matter if it's 10,000 years,
It's all my song, all my song.

The next two selections are typical examples of the "jail songs" craze of
1988-89, from Hei Taiyang's cassette, "Jail Songs: Educated Youth 68-69"
(*Qiuge,68-69 zhiqing*).

"Jail Song" (*Qiuge*)
music and lyrics: anonymous

Worries, worries, turned my hair white
When I left my parents, I went to live in the jail house

I can't stop my tears, down and down they flow
Being a hoodlum, a thief, I'm so ashamed
How can I lift my head?

In my hands I have a big hunk of steamed bread
I eat it, one bite follows the next
This lonely life is full of regrets
I'm so young, but I have no freedom
I can't stop my tears, down and down they flow

Thinking of the past kills me with pain
It's only today that I realize the shame
In this world, there's sweet wine and bitter
Better pay attention to which one you go after
So many girls gave up and jumped into the well
So many girls went to school and studied well
In this world, there's sweet wine and bitter
Better pay attention to which one you go after
If you bravely keep on trying,
You can turn your bitter wine sweet

"Song of an Educated Youth from Changchun" (*Changchun zhiqing ge*)
music: anonymous
lyrics: Duzi

I'm an educated youth
I was sent down to the country, to Jiutai county
All day I swung a pickaxe, digging shit for fertilizer
"Transforming the earth!" and "Changing the sky!"
Made me so tired my back and legs ached
After a year I was sent home
But I didn't even have any travelling money

Note: "Transform the earth" and "change the sky" were Maoist slogans popular during the years of the Cultural Revolution (1966-76), when many urban youths were sent to the countryside for ideological re-education through hard labor.

Rock music lyrics:

The following selections should convey something of the scope as well as recurrent themes to be found in rock lyrics as a whole. The first two songs are from the repertoire of the Breathing Band (*Huxi yuedui*), and are included on Wei Hua's *The Sun Rises*:

> "It's No Use Saying More" (*Bu yong zai duo shuo*)
> music: Gao Qi
> lyrics: Wei Hua, Gao Qi
>
> All of a sudden I was tired, tired of fooling myself
> All the smiles had already frozen, leaving only time
> I've cried, I've laughed, and in the end there was just one result
> Tell me where heaven's love song was finally lost
>
> I remember that I said I should face all this frustration
> I should see all the colors of humanity, now all that's left is deep sleep
> Awaken me, hold me tight, don't let me lose this moment
> We've already wasted too much, there's no use saying anything at all
>
> Give me silence, give me trials
> Give me arrogance, give me a little smile
> Give me a storm, give me wisdom
> Give me the end, give me a little bit of freedom
>
> All of a sudden I was tired, tired of fooling myself
> All the smiles had already frozen, leaving only time
> I've cried, I've laughed, and in the end there was just one result
> Tell me where heaven's love song was finally lost
>
> Give me silence, give me trials
> Give me arrogance, give me a little smile
> Give me a storm, give me wisdom
> Give me the end, give me a little bit of freedom
>
> "Wave Your Hands" (*Huiqi shou*)
> music: Gao Qi
> lyrics: Wei Hua, Gao Qi

I'm on top of the mountain yelling for you
You're shaking your head at the bottom of the mountain
Actually you're not willing to go, but you can't find an explanation
On top of the mountain there's a wind of freedom
You could ride the wind to the top
Stretch out your hand, come forward with me

Take a clear look around, where is the shining star of the past?
Why should you still bear that struggle, and all the ugliness?
Wave your hands, don't stay and look back
Wave your hands, follow my rhythm
Come with me, towards a new freedom, come with me

I've long had a fascination
For finding a world where I could fly
Grab my hand, we'll enjoy the feeling, you and I
These hands aren't flustered,
This heart lacks a little luster
Without you in this world
I'll be missing a little longing

Take a clear look around, where is the shining star of the past?
Why should you still bear that struggle, and all the ugliness?
Wave your hands, don't stay and look back
Wave your hands, follow my rhythm
Come with me

(*guitar solo*)

Take a clear look around, where is the shining star of the past?
Why should you still bear that struggle, and all the ugliness?
(*sung in English*)
Raise your hands, I want to see you raise them
Raise them high, try to touch the sky
Raise your hands, you've got to really want it
Raise your hands
Raise them up

The next selection, by the punk rocker He Yong, is distinctive for the violence and sexism of its imagery, as well as the satirical references to classical Chinese literature:

"Pretty Girl" (*Guniang piaoliang*)
music and lyrics: He Yong

Girl, girl
Pretty, pretty
Police, police
get out your guns
You say you want a car
You say you want a condominium
I can't rob
And I can't steal them

All I have is a squeaky bed
I can ride you on a bike to see the sunset
I have a delicious tongue for you to taste
I have a story
I want to tell you

Sun Wukong threw out his gold club and travelled overseas
Sandy the Monk stole a boat so he could catch all of the fish
Pigsy became a party director with women always giving him massages
Tang Xuan eats instant noodles on the street and tells people their fortunes

Girl, girl
Pretty, pretty
Police, police
Take out your guns
You say my story
Isn't a sausage
I know you can't
wear this sunset
I can't rob
And I can't steal it

Girl, girl

Pretty, pretty
Police, police
Take out your guns
You get into your car, step into your condo
You hold your baby
I still think of you
Should I find a girlfriend?
Better to take care of a dog!

Note: Sun Wukong, Sandy, Pigsy and Xuanzong are the principal characters in Wu Cheng'en's classic adventure story, Journey to the West (Xiyou ji).

The following selection can be found on Chang Kuan's *Making Plans for Now* (*Chongxin jihua xianzai*) album.

"City People" (*Chengli ren*)
music and lyrics: Chang Kuan

Never tasted rolls made of sorghum
Never drank water from a stone well
Never worn old cloth shoes
Never slept on a *kang* made of stone

I'm a young person in the city
Exhausted by the crowds streaming by
I'm thirsty for the peace of village life
I need the gentle rays of sunlight
I'm a young person in the city
Exhausted by the crowds of big buildings
I'm thirsty for the peace of village life
I need the gentle rays of sunlight

Taste a mouthful of sorghum bread, clean out my filthy stomach
Drink a gulp of clear, cool water, moisten my hoarse throat
Wear a pair or old cloth shoes, wander around the green mountains
Sleep on a warm earthen *kang*, heat up my frozen heart

Forget all the begging I do to make a living
Forget all the troubles of everyday living
Forget each and every cold face looking
Forget every bitter tear flowing

Note: A kang is heated brick platform bed common in northern Chinese peasant households.

The next two songs are performed by the heavy metal band Black Panthers (*Heibao*) on their eponymous debut album.

"Don't Come and Bother Me" (*Bie lai zuchan wo*)
music and lyrics: Dou Wei

I don't want to say anything more to you
Now you get the angry me
You've already drowned in your own hypocrisy
you've changed into an disgusting color

Do the work that you should do
better than all the rest
Change your ways so that others can stand you
You and I are equal, you and I

Hey! Don't come and bother me
Don't make me unhappy
This is a new China
I don't want to say more

How could all your talk be so arbitrary and rude
Is that what you call a rule?
Maybe you should do your politeness homework
Don't let people end up denouncing you out loud

Do the work that you should do
better than all the rest
Change your ways so that others can stand you
You and I are equal, you and I

Don't come and bother me
Don't make me unhappy
This is a new China
I don't want to say more

Don't come and bother me
Don't make me unhappy

This is a new China
I don't want to say more

Don't come and bother me--forget it
Don't make me unhappy
This is a new China
I don't want to say more

"Beijing Opera Mask" (*Lianpu*)
music and lyrics: Li Tong

Simple, simple thoughts
Rich, rich language
Foreign clothes, smiling face, starving eyes
but your heart is anxious
anxious to cry out

Living underneath
underneath hypocrisy
No one's ever looked at you twice
This is a realistic
this is a realistic place

Simple, simple thoughts
Rich, rich language
Foreign clothes, smiling face, starving eyes
but your heart is anxious
anxious to cry out

Living underneath
underneath hypocrisy
No one's ever looked at you twice
This is a realistic
this is a realistic place

Tearing open the hypocritical opera mask
You face this place
Choose once more a world of your own
Throw out your old shoes, get a brand new face
Only then will you find the world you're looking for

Simple, simple thoughts
Rich, rich language
Foreign clothes, smiling face, starving eyes
but your heart is anxious
anxious to cry out

Living underneath
underneath hypocrisy
No one's ever looked at you twice
This is a realistic
this is a realistic place

The final two selections are performed by the Tutu Band and taken from
their unreleased demo tape.

"Perhaps It's Always Been Wrong" (*Yexu conglai jiushi cuo*)
music: Zhu Xiaomin
lyrics: Da Ta

Always been that working isn't playing
Always been that in wartime it's the poor who are dying
Always been that ideals mean hoping and never getting
Always been that happiness is all memory and myth

Always been that fate's an uninvited guest
Always been that people have never seen Buddha or spirits
Always been that public opinion is just the world of truth
Always been that tradition is just a set of pretty handcuffs

(*repeat verse in double-time*)

Always always always been wrong...

Always been that ocean water just isn't for drinking
Always been that summer's hotter than spring
Always been that trees just aren't capable of thinking
Always been that horses and cows only heed people calling

Always been that humankind has shoulders but lacks wings

Always been that people just love asking why
Always been that people are just not used to seeing death as
returning
Always been that polite begging makes a living

(*repeat verse in double-time*)

Always always always been wrong...

"Broadcast Season" (*Chuanbo de jijie*)
music: Zhu Xiaomin
lyrics: Da Ta

If you're a writer of essays, then write with abandon
Piece by piece the letters spell out a new world
If you're painting a picture, then paint with freedom
The color and line in your brush can create something wild

If you're singing songs then sing out loud and plain
Sing sunlight into water, sing snow into rain
If you're brewing wine then put all you've got into brewing
See how many young girls and old men you can set reeling

If you're a flower, then go ahead and bloom quickly
Don't bother if you've bloomed badly or well, just do it warmly
If you're a dog, open up your throat and howl
Don't care if you howl at people, howl at the world, the sun, or the
moon

If you're a city then spread out like crazy
Don't mind that streets crowd together, buildings stream to the sky
If you're the sun and moon, then auction off your light and heat
Don't mind if it's summer or winter, day or night

If you're a dog then open your throat wide and howl
Don't care if you howl at people, howl at the world, the sun, or the
moon
If you're the sun and moon then auction off your light and heat
Don't mind if it's summer or winter, day or night

Note: Da Ta, the lyricist of the preceding two songs, is a minor poet of the "misty" school (menglong shipai).

BIBLIOGRAPHY

English language books and articles:

Adorno, Theodor W. "On Popular Music." In Simon Frith and Andrew Goodwin, eds. *On Record: Rock, Pop, and the Written Word.* New York: Pantheon Books, 1990.

Bakhtin, Mikhail. *Rabelais and His World.* Translated by Helen Iswolsky. Bloomington: Indiana University Press, 1984.

Barmé, Geremie. "Revolutionary Arias Sung to a New, Disco Beat." *Far Eastern Economic Review*, February 5, 1987: 36-8.

—. and John Minford, eds. *Seeds of Fire: Chinese Voices of Conscience.* New York: The Noonday Press, 1989.

—. and Linda Jaivin, eds. *New Ghosts, Old Dreams: Chinese Rebel Voices.* New York: Times Books, 1991.

Barthes, Roland. *Image, Music, Text.* New York: Hill and Wang, 1977.

Brace, Tim. "Popular Music in Contemporary Beijing: Modernism and Cultural Identity." *Asian Music* 2: 45-65 (Spring/Summer 1991).

Brake, Michael. *Comparative Youth Culture: The Sociology of Youth Cultures andYouth Subcultures in America, Britain, and Canada.* London: Routledge & Kegan Paul, 1985.

Chambers, Iain. "Some Critical Tracks." *Popular Music* 3: 19-36.

Chang, Won Ho. *Mass Media in China: The History and the Future.* Ames: Iowa State University Press, 1989.

Chen, Yusheng. "A Brand-New Music: Chinese Rock 'n' Roll." *Chinese Youth*, 1988/4: 30-1.

Chiu, Randy. "Disike Takes the Floor as Youth Culture Takes the Stage." *Far Eastern Economic Review*, 9 May, 1985: 61-2.

Chong, W.L. "Su Xiaokang on his Film 'River Elegy.'" *China Information* 3 (4): 44-55 (Winter 1989-90).

Chow, Rey. "Silent is the Ancient Plain: Music, Filmmaking, and the Conception of Reform in China's New Cinema." *Discourse* 12 (2): 82-109 (Spring-Summer 1989).

---. "Listening Otherwise, Music Miniaturized: A Different Type of Question About Revolution." *Discourse* 13 (2): 129-148 (Fall-Winter 1990-91).

Clark, Paul. *Chinese Cinema: Culture and Politics Since 1949.* Cambridge: Cambridge University Press, 1987.

Clarke, Gary. "Defending Ski-Jumpers: A Critique of Theories of Youth Subcultures." In Frith and Goodwin, eds. *On Record: Rock, Pop, and the Written Word.* New York: Pantheon Books, 1990.

Corbett, John. "Free, Single, and Disengaged: Listening Pleasure and the Popular Music Object." *October* 53: 79-101 (Winter 1991).

De Jong, Alice. "The Demise of the Dragon: Backgrounds to the Chinese Film 'River Elegy.'" *China Information* 3 (4): 28-43 (Winter 1989-90).

Delfs, Robert. "The Controversial Fame of China's First Rock Star." *Far Eastern Economic Review*, December 26, 1985.

Fitzgerald, Robert. "Deng's Development Drive and the Dawn of Decadence." *Far Eastern Economic Review*, April 5,1985.

Fraser, Nancy. *Unruly Practices: Power, Discourse, and Gender in Contemporary Social Theory.* Minneapolis: University of Minnesota Press, 1989.

—. "Rethinking the Public Sphere: A Contribution to the Critique of Actually Existing Democracy." *Social Text* 25/26: 56-80 (Winter 1990).

Friedlander, Paul David. "Rocking the Yangtze: Impressions of Chinese Popular Music and Technology." *Popular Music and Society* 1 (14): 62-74 (Spring 1990).

— "China's 'Newer Value' Pop: Rock-and-Roll and Technology on the New Long March." *Asian Music* 2: 67-81 (Spring/Summer 1991).

Frith, Simon. *Sound Effects: Youth, Leisure, and the Politics of Rock 'n' Roll.* New York: Pantheon Books, 1981.

—. "Towards an Aesthetic of Popular Music." In Richard Leppert and Susan McClary, eds. *Music and Society: The Politics of Composition, Performance and Reception*. Cambridge: Cambridge University Press, 1987: 133-150.

Gold, Thomas B. "Guerrilla Interviewing Among the *Getihu*." In Perry Link, Richard Madsen, Paul G. Pickowicz, eds. *Unofficial China: Popular Culture and Thought in the People's Republic*. Boulder: Westview Press, 1990.

Gramsci, Antonio. *Selections from the Prison Notebooks*. Edited and Translated by Quinten Hoare and Geoffrey Nowell Smith. London: Wishart, 1971.

Grossberg, Lawrence. "Is There Rock After Punk?" In Frith and Goodwin, eds. *On Record: Rock, Pop, and the Written Word*. New York: Pantheon Books, 1990.

Habermas, Jürgen. *The Structural Transformation of the Public Sphere: An Inquiry into a Category of Bourgeois Society*. Cambridge, MA: The MIT Press, 1989.

Hall, Stuart. "Encoding/Decoding." In Stuart Hall, et al., eds. *Culture, Media, Language*. London: Hutchison, 1980.

---. and Tony Jefferson, eds. *Resistance Through Rituals: Youth Subcultures in Post-war Britain*. London: Hutchison, 1976.

Hamm, Charles. "Music and Radio in the People's Republic of China." *Asian Music* 2: 1-42 (Spring/Summer 1991).

Hebdige, Dick. *Subculture: The Meaning of Style*. London: Routledge and Kegan Paul, 1987.

Horkheimer, Max, and Theodor W. Adorno. *Dialectic of Enlightenment*. New York: Continuum Books, 1988.

Human Rights in China. *Children of the Dragon: The Story of Tiananmen Square*. New York: Collier Books, 1990.

Huyssen, Andreas. *After the Great Divide: Modernism, Mass Culture, Postmodernism*. Bloomington: Indiana University Press, 1986.

Irving, Katrina. "Rock Music and the State: Dissonance or Counterpoint?" *Cultural Critique* 10: 151-170 (Fall 1988).

Jaivin, Linda. "Blowing His Own Trumpet." *Far Eastern Economic Review*, March 24, 1988: 84-87.

—. "Cultural Purge Sweeps Clean." *Far Eastern Economic Review*, August 23, 1990: 47-8.

—. "It's Only Rock and Roll, but China Likes It." *Asian Wall Street Journal*, October 12, 1990.

Jameson, Fredric. "Third-World Literature in the Era of Multinational Capitalism." *Social Text* 15: 65-87 (Fall 1986).

Johnson, David, Andrew Nathan, and Evelyn S. Rawski, eds. *Popular Culture in Late Imperial China*. Berkeley: University of California Press, 1985.

Kristof, Nicholas D. "Stilled by the Unthinkable, a Singer Tries His Voice." *New York Times*, January 16, 1990.

—. "Fear Abates Among Chinese but Few Find Cause for Hope." *New York Times*, November 24, 1990.

Liberati, Patrizia. "Shouting from the Mountain Tops." *China Now* 130: 34-5.

Liu, Zaifu. "Chinese Literature in the Past Ten Years: Spirit and Direction." Translated by Stephen Fleming. *Chinese Literature*, Autumn 1989: 151-77.

Lull, James, ed. *Popular Music and Communication*. Newbury Park: Sage Publications, 1987.

---. *China Turned On: Television, Reform, and Resistance*. London and New York: Routledge, 1991.

McDougall Bonnie, ed. *Popular Chinese Literature and Performing Arts in the People's Republic of China, 1949-79*. Berkeley: University of California Press, 1988.

—. *Mao Zedong's Talks at the Yan'an Conference on Literature and Art*. Ann Arbor: University of Michigan Press, 1980.

MacFarquhar, Emily. "Back to the Future in China." *U.S. News and World Report*, March 12, 1990: 40-45.

Manuel, Peter Lamarche. *Popular Musics of the Non-Western World: An Introductory Survey*. New York: Oxford University Press, 1988.

Mao, Bian. "How a TV Contest Captivated China: Music Lesson For Millions." *Chinese Youth*, 1987/1: 28-30.

Miao, Junjie. "A Preliminary Study of Literary Schools in the New Era." *Chinese Literature*, Winter 1988: 174-85.

Minford, John. "Picking Up the Pieces." *Far Eastern Economic Review*, August 8, 1985: 30-32.

Nettl, Bruno. *The Western Impact on World Music*. New York: Schirmer Books, 1985.

Owen, Stephen. "Selections from the *Record of Music*." With translation and commentary. Unpublished manuscript.

Pen American Center. "Chinese Writers Under Fire: The Struggle for Human Rights in China." Transcript of a panel discussion with Duo Duo, Perry Link, Arthur Miller, Robin Munro, Orville Schell, Shen Tong, Jonathan Spence, Su Wei. *Pen American Center Newsletter* 70: 15-23 (December 1989).

Perris, Arnold. "Music as Propaganda: Art at the Command of Doctrine in the People's Republic of China." *Ethnomusicology*, 17/1: :1-28 (1983).

Polan, Dana. "The Public's Fear, or Media as Monster in Habermas, Negt, and Kluge." *Social Text* 25/26: 260-66 (Winter 1990).

Poll Work Group, Psychology Department, Beijing Normal University. "Beijing Public Opinion Poll on the Student Demonstrations." Translated by Woei Lien Chong and Fons Lamboo. China Information 1 (4): 94-124 (Summer 1989).

Pratt, Ray. *Rhythm and Resistance: Explorations in the Political Uses of Popular Music*. New York: Praeger, 1990.

Scott, A.C. *Literature and the Arts in 20th Century China*. Gloucester, MA: Peter Smith, 1968.

Scott, James C. *Domination and the Arts of Resistance: Hidden Transcripts*. New Haven: Yale University Press, 1990.

Shen, Tong. *Almost a Revolution*. With Marianne Yen. Boston: Houghton Mifflin, 1990.

Shephard, John. "Music and Male Hegemony." In Richard Leppert and Susan McClary, eds. *Music and Society: The Politics of*

Composition, Performance and Reception. Cambridge: Cambridge University Press, 1987.

Street, John. *Rebel Rock: The Politics of Popular Music*. New York: Basil Blackwell, 1986.

Tong, Wei. "Rock 'n' Roll China." *Nexus: China in Focus*, Summer 1990: 14-21.

Turner, Victor. *The Ritual Process: Structure and Anti-Structure*. Chicago: Aldine Publishing Company, 1969.

—. *The Anthropology of Performance*. New York: PAJ Publications, 1986.

Wicke, Peter. *Rock Music: Culture, Aesthetics, and Sociology*. Cambridge: Cambridge University Press, 1987.

Yau, Esther. "*Yellow Earth*: Western Analysis and a Non-Western Text." *Film Quarterly* 2 (41): 22-33 (Winter 1987-88).

Zhang, Yingjin. "Ideology of the Body in Red Sorghum: National Allegory, National Roots, and Third Cinema." *East-West Film Journal* 2 (4): 38-51 (June 1990).

Zheng, Yong. "Breakdancing Whirlwind." *Chinese Youth*, 1988/5: 34-6.

Chinese language books and articles:

A Bing. "Cui Jian: dangjin Zhongguo touhao yaogun yue gexing" [Cui Jian: contemporary China's first rock and roll star]. *Yinyue aihaozhe*, 1988/2: 32.

Bai Jieming. "Yaogun fanshen le?" [Has rock stood up?]. *Jiushi niandai*, 1988/11: 94-5.

Bei Fangshuo. "Dalu yaogun yue he Cui Jian xianxiang" [Mainland rock music and the Cui Jian phenomena]. *Kaifang*, 1991/3: 88-89.

Bo Yinchu. "Tan 'huangtu re'" [Discussing the "yellow earth fever"]. *Renmin yinyue*, 1989/2: 27.

Chen Di. "Dui liuxing yinyue de guance" [Observations on popular music]. *Yinyue yanjiu*, 1986/3: 51-60.

Chen Zhi'ang. "Liuxing yinyue pipan" [A critique of popular music]. *Yinyue yanjiu*, 1989/4: 14-20.

Cheng Yun. "Zhongguo dangdai tongsu yinyue huanshi lu" [An overview of contemporary Chinese popular music]. *Renmin yinyue*, 1988/2:

---. "Dui tongsu yinyue wenti de sikao" [Thoughts on the problem of *tongsu* music]. *Chun zhi sheng*, 1985/8: 23-4.

Duan Ruanzhong. "Jigong 'Huangtu gaopo'" [An Attack on "Hills of Yellow Earth"]. *Renmin yinyue*, 1989/3: 30-1.

Editors of *Yinyue Yanjiu*. "Tan liuxing yinyue" [Discussing popular music]. *Yinyue yanjiu*, 1988/3: 16-24.

Fan Weiqiang. "Rang Zhongguo de tongsu gequ zouxiang shijie" [Let Chinese popular music go towards the world]. *Yinyue wudao yanjiu*, 1987/11: 27-30.

Fang Jianjun. "Zhongguo xibu yaogun yue zhi xingqi" [The rise of Chinese western rock music]. *Yinyue bolan*, 1988/2: 23-4.

Gao Guojun and Jun Bo. *Yaogun de getan* [The rocking pop music scene]. Hangzhou: Zhejiang wenyi chubanshe, 1989.

Gu Tu. "Cong 'Yiwu suoyou' shuodao yaogun yue: Cui Jian de zuopin weishenme shou huanying?" [From 'I have nothing' to rock music: why have Cui Jian's works become popular?]. *Renmin ribao*, July 16, 1988.

Guo Zhaosheng. "Xiechu Zhongguo tese de liuxing gequ lai" [Create a popular music with Chinese characteristics]. *Yinyue tiandi*, 1987/4: 27-8.

Hu Yinsheng. "Dui tongsu gequ disu xianxiang de sikao" [Thoughts on the phenomenon of vulgar *tongsu* music]. *Yinyue tiandi*, 1990/3: 23.

Hua Yan, ed. *'Heshang' pipan* [Criticizing *River Elegy*]. Beijing: Wenhua yishu chubanshe, 1989.

Huang Baolian. "Dalu yaogun yue jianchi yinyue geming" [Mainland rock music steadfastly revolutionizes music]. *Zhongguo shibao zhoukan*, April 26, 1992: 58.

Jin Zhaojun. "Feng cong nali lai: ping getan 'xibei feng'" [Where's the wind coming from: on popular music's "Northwest Wind"]. *Renmin ribao*, August 23, 1988.

—. "Cui Jian yu Zhongguo yaogun yue" [Cui Jian and Chinese rock music]. *Renmin yinyue*, 1989/4: 32-3.

—. "Liuxing yinyue: duanxiang sanze" [Popular music: three conclusions]. *Gequ*, 1989/9: 28-30.

—. "Shehui yinyue wenhua zai 1990" [Musical culture and society in 1990]. *Gongren ribao*, January 1, 1990.

Ju Qihong. "Zhenshi renxing de fugui yu shenghua: tongsu gequ zhi renwen jiazhi yu bu zu" [The resurgence and flowering of true human nature: the humanistic values and inadequacies of *tongsu* songs]. *Cikan*, 1989/7: 30-32.

Lao Mu, ed. *Xin shichao shiji* [Collected poems of the new wave]. Two volumes. Beijing: Beijing Daxue wusi wenxue she Weiming Hu congshu bianweihui, 1985.

Li Enchun. "Lun 'xibeifeng' de xuanlu yu jiezou tedian" [On the melodic and rhythmic characteristics of the "Northwest Wind"]. *Renmin yinyue*, 1990/2: 34-5.

Li Tianyi. "Tongsu yinyue heyuan luoru digu" [What caused popular music's decline?]. *Renmin yinyue*, 1989/11: 27.

Liang Maochun. "Dui woguo liuxing yinyue lishi de sikao" [Thoughts on the history of Chinese popular music]. *Renmin yinyue*,1988/7: 32-34.

Lie Fu, ed. *Wo shi yi ba daozi: Cui Jian* [Cui Jian: I am a knife]. Hong Kong: Pan China Media Ltd., 1991.

Ling Xuan. "'Xibei feng' yu 'Qiuge'" [The "Northwest Wind" and "Jail Songs"]. *Renmin yinyue*, 1989/5: 37-8.

Liu Jian. "Xiandai ren de shengming nahan: lun dangdai chengshi minge xinchao" [A cry of life for modern people: on the new wave of contemporary urban folk song]. *Renmin yinyue*, 1990/2: 32-34.

Liu Suola. "Duoyu de gushi" [A superfluous story]. *Shouhuo*, 1986/2: 110-116.

Liu Wei and Shi Jie, eds. *Yiwu suoyou: liuxing gequ ji* [I have nothing: a collection of popular songs]. Wuhan: Changjiang wenyi chubanshe, 1988.

Liu Yiran. "Yaogun qingnian" [Rock and roll youth]. *Qingnian wenxue*, 1988/10: 4-28.

Liu Zhenbang. "Fandui 'Jigong Huangtu gaopo'" [Against "An Attack on 'Hills of Yellow Earth'"]. *Renmin yinyue*, 1989/8: 24-5.

Ma Dongfeng. "Lai ye congcong, qu ye congcong: tongsu getan xiankuang pouxi yu sikao" [Easy come, easy go: analysis and ideas on the current state of the popular music scene]. *Yinyue shenghuo*, 1990/3: 3-4.

Mao Sen. "Fanpan wenhua, dalu de yaogun yi zu: fang 'Xieran de fengcai' zuoci ren Chen Zhe" [Rebellious culture, mainland rock: an interview with the lyricist of 'The blood stained spirit,' Chen Zhe]. *Jiushi niandai*, 1991/9: 72-75.

Miao Ye. "Zai kaifang de chaoliu zhong qiu fazhan: dui woguo tongsu yinyue chuangzuo wenti de sikao" [Seeking development in the midst of opening up to the outside world: thoughts on the question of artistic production in China's popular music]. *Renmin ribao*, January 5, 1988.

Mu Mu. "Tianbian gunlai de gesheng" [The sound rolling down from the sky]. *Qingnian yuekan*, 1990/5: 17-21.

Ping Fang and Ma Mu. "Yiwu suoyou, yaogun yu touji: wei Yayun hui juankuan yibaiwan yuan yiyan jishi" [I have nothing, rock and opportunism: a record of Cui Jian's tour to raise one million *yuan* for the Asian Games]. *Xiju shijie*, 1990/3-4: 2-11.

Ren Zhen. "Cui Jian he Zhongguo yaogun chao" [Cui Jian and China's rock wave]. *Caifeng bao*, August 8, 1990.

Shi Han. "'Bu shi wo bu zhidao': qingnian geshou Liu Huan caifang lu" ["It's not that I don't understand": an interview with young singer Liu Huan]. In Tian Qing, ed. *Zhongguo yinyue nianjian 1988* [China music yearbook 1988]. Beijing: Wenhua yishu chubanshe, 1989.

Shi Yi. "Dianying 'Hong gaoliang' jiqi fankui" [The film *Red Sorghum* and its feedback]. *Dianying dianshi yishu yanjiu*, 1988/8: 47-51.

Song Ling and Jiang Tao. "La Cui Jian" [Interviewing Cui Jian]. *Qingnian yuekan*, 1990/5: 22-23.

Song Yang. "Tongsu gequ de minzu xing" [The national character of *tongsu* songs]. *Renmin yinyue*, 1988/6: 26-8.

Su Xiaokang and Wang Luxiang. *Heshang* [River elegy]. Hong Kong: Joint Publishing Co.,1988.

Tang He. "Cong 'tongsu yinyue' lai tan yinyue de tongsu xing" [Discussing the popular nature of music through popular music]. *Yinyue wudao yanjiu*, 1986/3: 7-10.

Wang Yanqi and Han Xiaohui, eds. *Dangdai gewang* [Contemporary kings of song]. Beijing: Huafu chubanshe, 1989.

Wang Yongling. "'Xibu gequ' re chuxian hou de li yu bi" [After the appearance of a 'Western Song' fever: an appraisal]. *Renmin yinyue*, 1989/6: 31.

Xiao Hui. "Yaogun, renge, ji qita: jian lun Cui Jian men de yinyue" [Rock, morality, and more: appraising the music of Cui Jian and his contemporaries]. *Yishu guangjiao*, 1988/94-6.

Xu Bing. "Shan dandan yu yaogun yue: tongsu gequ 'Xintianyou' ji qita" [Mountain lilies and rock music: the *tongsu* song "Xintianyou" and more]. *Yinyue aihaozhe*, 1987/5: 31.

Yang Duanqing. "Tongsu xinge zai shenian" [New *tongsu* songs in the year of the snake]. *Yinyue shenghuo*, 1990/3: 3-4.

Yang Wenyong, ed. *Zhongguo gexing gequ lu* [Chinese pop stars and pop songs]. Two volumes. Beijing: Dongfang chubanshe, 1990.

Yin Hui. "Beijing yaogun yue sheng sheng bu xi" [Beijing rock won't quit]. *Zhongguo shibao zhoukan*, April 26, 1992: 60-62.

Yu Liangxin. "Zouchu ziwo tanxi de xiao tiandi: tan tongsu gequ de xianzhuang ji fazhan" [Leaving the limited realm of self-pity: on the current state and development of *tongsu* songs]. *Cikan*, 1989/7: 32-33.

Yuan Kun and Chun Hua. "Shinian getan: gequ da liuxing" [Ten years of music: the rise of popular song]. *Qingnian yuekan*,1989/10: 13-15.

Zhang Fei. "Zai quanguo tongsu yinyue yantaohui shang de bimuci" [Closing remarks at the national conference on *tongsu* music]. *Renmin yinyue*, 1988/1: 2-6.

Zhang Guangsheng. "Tongsu gequ de minzu xing" [The national character of *tongsu* songs]. *Yinyue shenghuo*, 1987/10: 3-4.

Zhang Hailong and Zhang Li. "Cong 'Meimei ni dadande wang qian zou' xiangdao de: tan yinyue jianshang yu sixiang zhengzhi gongzuo" [Thinking from 'Sister, go bravely forward': on music appreciation and ideological education work]. *Yinyue shenghuo*, 1989/7: 3-4.

Zheng Xiangqun. "Yaobai yue jiqi tezheng" [Rock music and its characteristics]. *Renmin yinyue*, 1988/7: 42-3.

Zhong Lu. "Hou Dejian tan liuxing yinyue" [Hou Dejian discusses popular music]. *Qing yinyue*, 1985/2: 20-1.

Zhu Xingyi, Ge Guang, Qiao Guoliang. "Zou xue! zou xue!" [Going to the cave! Going to the cave!]. In Si Shui, ed. *Shehui wenti chensi lu: baogao wenxue xuan* [Serious considerations of social problems: an anthology of literary reportage]. Beijing: Renmin wenxue chubanshe, 1990.

DISCOGRAPHY

Collections of *Tongsu* Music:

Assorted artists. *Bei xiangei de yidai: Wenge zhiqing zhenzang geji* [The sacrificed generation: treasured songs of the educated youth of the Cultural Revolution]. Shantou yinxiang chubanshe HLS-298,1990.

---. *Beijing reggae.* Golden Pony Records GPL-1003-2

---. *Chenxing bainian* [The stars celebrate the new year]. Wuhan yinxiang chubanshe DS-8820, 1990.

---. *Dongfang hong yaogun* [East is red rock]. Zhongguo luyin luxiang chubanshe BB-48, 1989.

---. *Fantian fudi: Zhongguo xin yinyue xilie zhi er* [The world is overturned: Chinese new waves volume 2]. Yongsheng yinyue chuban youxian gongsi SMC-90002, 1990.

---. *Guaxiang 89 de da xuanfeng* [The whirlwind of 1989]. Zhongguo qingnian yinxiang chubanshe QN-063, 1989.

---. *Hei yueliang: ling yishuang yan kan Zhongguo* [Black moon: the other side of China]. CZ Music Production ACD-1, 1991.

---. *Hong gaoliang* [Red sorghum]. Guangxi minzu shengxiang yishu chubanshe AB-1001, 1988.

---. *Huangtu gaopo* [Hills of yellow earth]. Tianjin yinxiang youxian gongsi DF-1209, 1988.

---. *Qingge pili 88* [Easy listening, break dance, 88]. Yangzijiang yinxiang chubanshe Q-078, 1990.

---. *Jin mu shui huo tu: Zhongguo wu da yaogun chenxing* [Gold, wood, water, fire, earth: China's five greatest rock stars]. Zhongguo luyou shengxiang chubanshe, 1989.

---. *Kaitian pidi: Zhongguo xin yinyue xilie zhi yi* [The window is opened: Chinese new waves volume 1]. Yongsheng yinyue chuban youxian gongsi SWC-8250, 1989.

---. *Liba nüren gou* [Twig fence, woman, dog]. Zhongguo qingnian yinxiang chubanshe QN-044, 1990.

---. *Midi* [The answer to the riddle]. Zhongguo dianying chubanshe J106-125, 1990.

---. *Shanbei 1988* [Northwest wind 1988]. Zhongguo dianying chubanshe J-0134, 1988.

---. *Xuese de huanghun '88* [Blood red dusk '88]. Zhongguo heping yinxiang chubanshe SY-015, 1988.

---. *Yaogun xianfeng* [Rock pioneers]. Zhongguo luyin luxiang chuban zongshe BB-57, 1988.

---. *Yazhou xiongfeng: di shiyi ju Yayun hui gequ* [The valiant spirit of Asia: songs of the 11th Asian Games]. Zhongguo guangbo yinxiang chubanshe BM-025, 1990.

---. *Zhongguo xiangtu yaogun* [Chinese country rock]. Guangdong yinxiang chubanshe GY-114, 1990.

---. *Zhongguo xinan gehui* [Southwest China concert]. Sichuan sheng yinxiang chubanshe SC-L0115, 1990.

Recordings of individual *tongsu* singers:

Ai Jing. *Ai Jing zhuanji: qingdou chukai* [Collected songs of Ai Jing: awakening of love]. Hubei yinxiang chubanshe EVA-8832, 1988.

Hei Taiyang. *Qiuge: 68-69 zhiqing* [Jail songs: educated youth of 68-69], Liaoning beiguo yinxiang chubanshe DF-1241, 1989.

Na Ying. *Renbuzhu kan ta* [I can't help looking at him]. Yangzijiang yinxiang chubanshe Q-131, 1990.

Sun Guoqing. *Sun Guoqing zhuanji: xiangei Yayun hui* [Collected songs of Sun Guoqing: dedicated to the Asian Games]. Zhongguo beiguang shengxiang yishu gongsi BSL-10, 1990.

Tian Zhen. *Milu nühai* [The lost girl]. Wenhua yishu chubanshe WG-048, 1989.

Tu Honggang. *Tu Honggang zhuanji: yuanshi yipi lang* [Collected songs of Tu Honggang: it was a wolf]. Zhongguo luyin luxiang zongshe TKBB-047,1990.

Wang Hong. *Xieran de fengcai* [The blood stained spirit]. Yuesheng changpian gongsi MRCS-8026, 1989.

Zhang Yanni. *Zhang Yanni zhuanji* [Collected songs of Zhang Yanni]. Taipingyang yinxiang gongsi P-2103, 1984.

Zhang Yimou. *Yaogun hong gaoliang* [Rocking red sorghum]. Zhejiang yinxiang chubanshe ZL-156, 1988.

Recordings of Chinese Rock Music:

Chang Kuan. *Chongxin jihua xianzai* [Making plans for now]. EMI/Dadi FH-500784, 1990.

Cui Jian. *Xin changzheng lushang de yaogun* [New long march rock]. Zhongguo luyou yinxiang chubanshe BJZ-01, 1989.

---. *Yiwu suoyou* [I have nothing]. EMI CDFH-50037, 1989.

---. *Langzi gui* [The wanderer returns]. BMG/Current 8.280031, 1989.

---. *Jiejue* [Solution]. EMI FX 500762, 1991.

---. *Jiejue* [Solution]. Zhongguo beiguang shengxiang yishu gongsi BSL-029, 1991

Heibao. *Heibao* [Black Panthers]. Kinn's Management LTD. KM91-2-02, 1991.

Wei Hua. *Taiyang sheng* [The sun rises]. RCA/BMG Pacific 8.280048, 1990.

Recordings of popular music from Taiwan and Hong Kong:

Deng Lijun. *Gaobie getan jinqu* [Farewell to the music world: golden hits]. Zhongguo guangbo luyin chubanshe BM-005, 1990.

---. *Greatest Hits Vol.3*. Polygram Records 3199-321, 1982.

Hou Dejian. *Hou Dejian zuopin xuan* [Selected works of Hou Dejian]. Chuansheng changpian gongsi PSC-9001, 1990.

---. *Sanshi sui yihou* [After thirty]. Chuansheng changpian gongsi PSLP-3904, 1988.

Luo Dayou. *Airen tongzhi* [Comrade lover]. BMG Pacific RC-1001, 1990.

---. *Lianqu 1980-1990* [Love songs, 1980-1990]. Beijing yinxiang gongsi YY90-01, 1990.

Qi Qin. *Lang* [Wolf]. Guoji wenhua jiaoliu yinxiang chubanshe IBC-88002, 1988.

Zhao Chuan. *Wo hen chou, keshi wo hen wenrou* [I'm very ugly, but I'm very gentle]. Beijing shi qing shaonian yinxiang chubanshe BQY-9003, 1990.

Live concert recordings:

Cui Jian. Performance at Beijing Exhibition Hall, Beijing, March 12, 1989.

---. Performance at Ritan Park, Beijing, July 8, 1990.

He Yong. Performance at Ritan Park, Beijing, July 8, 1990.

Heibao yuedui [Black Panthers]. Performance at the Restaurant for Foreign Diplomatic Missions, Beijing, June 16, 1990.

Huxi yuedui [Breathing Band]. Performance at the Restaurant for Foreign Diplomatic Missions, Beijing, June 16, 1990.

Tutu yuedui [Tutu Band]. Performance at Ritan Park, Beijing, July 8, 1990.

CORNELL EAST ASIA SERIES

No.   2   *China's Green Revolution*, by Benedict Stavis

No.   4   *Provincial Leadership in China: The Cultural Revolution and Its Aftermath*, by Fredrick Teiwes

No.   8   *Vocabulary and Notes to Ba Jin's Jia: An Aid for Reading the Novel*, by Cornelius C. Kubler

No. 14   *Black Crane 1: An Anthology of Korean Literature*, edited by David R. McCann

No. 15   *Song, Dance, Storytelling: Aspects of the Performing Arts in Japan*, by Frank Hoff

No. 16   *Nō as Performance: An Analysis of the Kuse Scene of Yamamba*, by Monica Bethe and Karen Brazell (videotapes available)

No. 17   *Pining Wind: A Cycle of Nō Plays*, translated by Royall Tyler

No. 18   *Granny Mountains: A Second Cycle of Nō Plays*, translated by Royall Tyler

No. 21   *Three Works by Nakano Shigeharu*, translated by Brett de Bary

No. 22   *The Tale of Nezame: Part Three of Yowa no Nezame Monogatari*, translated by Carol Hochstedler

No. 23   *Nanking Letters, 1949*, by Knight Biggerstaff

No. 25   *Four Japanese Travel Diaries of the Middle Ages*, translated by Herbert Plutschow and Hideichi Fukuda

No. 27   *The Jurchens in the Yüan and Ming*, by Morris Rossabi

No. 28   *The Griffis Collection of Japanese Books: An Annotated Bibliography*, edited by Diane E. Perushek

No. 29   *Dance in the Nō Theater*, by Monica Bethe and Karen Brazell
       Volume 1:   Dance Analysis
       Volume 2:   Plays and Scores
       Volume 3:   Dance Patterns
   (videotapes available)

No. 30   *Irrigation Management in Japan: A Critical Review of Japanese Social Science Research*, by William W. Kelly

No. 31   *Water Control in Tokugawa Japan: Irrigation Organization in a Japanese River Basin, 1600-1870*, by William W. Kelly

No. 32   *Tone, Segment, and Syllable in Chinese: A Polydimensional Approach to Surface Phonetic Structure*, by A. Ronald Walton

No. 35   *From Politics to Lifestyles: Japan in Print, I*, edited by Frank Baldwin

No. 36   *The Diary of a Japanese Innkeeper's Daughter*, translated by Miwa Kai, edited and annotated by Robert J. Smith and Kazuko Smith

No. 37   *International Perspectives on Yanagita Kunio and Japanese Folklore Studies*, edited by J. Victor Koschmann, Ōiwa Keibō and Yamashita Shinji

No. 38   *Murō Saisei: Three Works*, translated by James O'Brien

No. 40   *Land of Volcanic Ash: A Play in Two Parts by Kubo Sakae*, translated by David G. Goodman

No. 41   *The Dreams of Our Generation and Selections from Beijing's People*, by Zhang Xinxin, edited and translated by Edward Gunn, Donna Jung and Patricia Farr

No. 43   *Post-War Japanese Resource Policies and Strategies: The Case of Southeast Asia*, by Shoko Tanaka

No. 44   *Family Change and the Life Course in Japan*, by Susan Orpett Long

No. 45   *Regulatory Politics in Japan: The Case of Foreign Banking*, by Louis W. Pauly

No. 46   *Planning and Finance in China's Economic Reforms*, by
         Thomas P. Lyons and WANG Yan

No. 48   *Bungo Manual: Selected Reference Materials for Students of
         Classical Japanese*, by Helen Craig McCullough

No. 49   *Ankoku Butō: The Premodern and Postmodern Influences on
         the Dance of Utter Darkness*, by Susan Blakeley Klein

No. 50   *Twelve Plays of the Noh and Kyōgen Theaters*, edited by
         Karen Brazell

No. 51   *Five Plays by Kishida Kunio*, edited by David Goodman

No. 52   *Ode to Stone*, by Shirō Hara, translated by James Morita

No. 53   *Defending the Japanese State: Structures, Norms and the
         Political Responses to Terrorism and Violent Social Protest in
         the 1970s and 1980s*, by Peter Katzenstein and Yutaka
         Tsujinaka

No. 54   *Deathsong of the River: A Reader's Guide to the Chinese TV
         Series* Heshang, by Su Xiaokang and Wang Luxiang,
         translated by Richard W. Bodman and Pin P. Wan

No. 55   *Psychoanalysis in China: Literary Transformations, 1919-
         1949*, by Jingyuan Zhang

No. 56   *To Achieve Security and Wealth: The Qing Imperial State and
         the Economy, 1644-1911*, edited by Jane Kate Leonard and
         John Watt

No. 57   *Like a Knife: Ideology and Genre in Contemporary Chinese
         Popular Music*, by Andrew F. Jones

For ordering information, please contact the *Cornell East Asia Series*, East
Asia Program, Cornell University, 140 Uris Hall, Ithaca, NY 14853-7601
USA, (607) 255-6222.

10-92/.6M/BB